Get your public speaking mojo back forever!

50 imaginative ideas to help you

communicate with confidence

**Britain's Next
BESTSELLER**

First published in 2014 by:

Britain's Next Bestseller
An imprint of Live It Publishing
27 Old Gloucester Road
London, United Kingdom.
WC1N 3AX

www.britainsnextbestseller.co.uk

Copyright © 2014 by Julie Howell

The moral right of Julie Howell to be identified as the author
of this work has been asserted by her in accordance with the
Copyright, Designs and Patents Act 1988.

All rights reserved.

Except as permitted under current legislation, no part of this
work may be photocopied, stored in a retrieval system,
published, performed in public, adapted, broadcast, transmitted,
recorded or reproduced in any form or by any means, without
the prior permission of the copyright owners.

All enquiries should be addressed to Britain's Next Bestseller.

ISBN 978-1-906954-87-1

"An inspiring book that crystallises the core lessons in an unforgettable way. Tells you the things you really need to know, especially when it comes to the hard, tedious stuff like rehearsing, and doesn't pull any punches."
BILL THOMPSON, BBC WORLD SERVICE

"Rich in insight. Lifts the lid on the reality of public speaking."
RASHEED OGUNLARU, SPEAKER,
LIFE COACH AND AUTHOR

"Hugely appealing. I found myself swept along by Julie's positive and confident voice and thoroughly engaged by the simple yet effective practical exercises."
SAM DAVIES, DIRECTOR OF PHILANTHROPY & ALUMNI
ENGAGEMENT, UNIVERSITY OF BRIGHTON

"A powerful tool for beginners and experts alike, providing insights from a lifetime of practical experience."
DEAN RUSSELL, ST ALBANS DISTRICT COUNCILLOR
FOR HARPENDEN EAST

"Inspired and inspiring. Julie's advice and exercises will help you become a better public speaker by getting you to think about the impact you want to have, as well as how to achieve it."
PHILIP SMITH, HAYMARKET BUSINESS MEDIA

Get Your Public Speaking Mojo Back Forever
Supporters list

Paul Bolland, Helen Savage, Ollie Bolland, Amy Bolland, Josh Bolland, Kris Croucher, Maria Ward, David Stevenson, Stuart & Theresa Stevenson, Claudio Concha, Shar Platt, Julie Smith, Natalie Wills, Victoria Norris-Jones, Julie Patricia Davies, Martin Gladdish, Peter Abrahams, David Sloan, Ian Stuart, Chris Day, Alison Ward, Anne Murray, David Rhys Wilton, Mark Sherwin, Calum Williamson, Christina Christou, Nicola Lambert, Angharad Rees, Laura Bassinder, Denise Hudson, Julian Roland, Jo McMahon, Matthew Lyons, Diane Goldman, Abby Dennis, Jos Creese, Jonathan Hassell, Andy Whyte, Dr Phil Friend OBE, Paul Blunden, Justin Pearse, Richard Leader, Louise Croft Baker, Steve Green, Dr David Kreps, Chris Russell, Michelle Fuller, Jim Barter, Paul Crichton, Steve Lee, Felix Velarde, Ben Logan, Michael Krausz, Gill Whitney, Sheila Williamson, Rob Hazlem, Owen Valentine Pringle, Nick Lansley, Lynn Wadsworth, Master Mike, Mark Lewis, Phil Strachan – Strangebrew, Nimesh Manmohanlal, Brendan Hamley, Omaid Hiwaizi, Martin Kliehm, Alasdair Scott, David Matheson, Becky Slack, Patricia, Nauzar Manekshaw – Branduin, E.A. Draffan, Laura Simmons, Amanda Neylon, Tony Hudson, Paul Chandler, Michael Elders, Tom Wood, Graham Armfield, Lisa Halabi, Caroline Jarrett, Rob Bonn, Dean Russell, Jon Rimmer, Tom Cannon, Jason Wilburn, Sean McManus, Sheena Roberts, James Buller, Peter Bosher, Melonie Isaacs, Paul Isaacs, Sir Bernard Goldman, Amanda Searle, Justin Cooke, Harry Loots, Joyce 'JoGreenDragon' Howarth, Garry Hunter, Christina Clark-Tietjen, Julie Curtis, Marrying Later in Life, Ian & Tina Bruce, Anne Ferrier, Robin Spinks, Software Acumen, Sam Davies, Christine Lunney, Sheila Acayo, Angus Grady, Gary Fullwood, Anne Clark, Carl Moorhouse, Stuart Doughton, Vincent Madden, Emma Howie, Julie Marah, Li Webster, Louise Ferguson Bilbao, Chris Ellis, David Deutsch, Rod Milicevic, Mag Leahy, Ian Welland, Charity Times, Guido Gybels, Tanis Mills, Paul Hoskins, Graham Meehan, Alby Atkinson, Day Media, Ian Wilkinson, Chaals, Antonia Chitty, Eleanor Lisney, Graeme Aymer, Richard Dinnick, Adele Long, Giles M S Barker, Brian Hardy, Jon Nolan, Dennis Kessler, Martin Maguire, Dan Jellinek, Dane Wright, Gabrielle Stirling, Chris Bray and Keri Lambden.

Contents

Exercises by Chapter

A video to accompany each exercise is available at www.publicspeakingmojo.co.uk You need a password to access the video page. This is it: **h3110m0j0**

You are not alone (everyone does it!)
GIVE IT A GO! #1 Does it matter?

Re-frame your 'bad' experience
GIVE IT A GO! #2 How they describe me

When bad things happen to good speakers
GIVE IT A GO! #3 It only takes one person to change the world
GIVE IT A GO! #4 Judging yourself
GIVE IT A GO! #5 Happy thoughts

Why that great advice your family gave you isn't so great
GIVE IT A GO! #6 Bad advice!
GIVE IT A GO! #7 Noticing negativity
GIVE IT A GO! #8 A thankful mindset

Change means growth (and growth hurts!)
GIVE IT A GO! #9 Say 'Yes'
GIVE IT A GO! #10 What do you do?

We can be heroes: why it is your duty to perform
GIVE IT A GO! #11 Your valuable knowledge
GIVE IT A GO! #12 Whose voice do you hear?
GIVE IT A GO! #13 Antmusic!
GIVE IT A GO! #14 A lesson in 'channelling'

For Elizabeth Telford, who loved words and would have loved these words in particular.

1918–2013

About the author

Julie Howell is not a natural public speaker. Just like you, she's had to work at it.

Born in Hampshire, England in 1971, Julie had no interest in public speaking until 1997, when an insightful manager coerced her into making her first public presentation. On discovering the joy (and the power) of public speaking she vowed never to look back and now has an unshakeable belief that public speaking is a set of skills that anyone can learn.

A tenacious and influential disability rights campaigner, writer and successful speaking and confidence coach Julie has a passion for making things happen and no time for naysayers ('If I had accepted what other people say is possible I wouldn't have achieved very much at all'). She holds five major awards for her work as a mentor, campaigner and digital pioneer.

Julie has a degree in Library and Information Studies from Brighton Polytechnic. In 2012, she became Brighton University's inaugural Alumnus of the Year in recognition of her work in the community and her mentoring support of several of the University's female undergraduates.

Julie has appeared on every major British TV channel and spoken at events around the globe, taking in China, Canada and the United Arab Emirates. She lives (with an assortment of cantankerous and demanding rescue cats) in the village of Abbots Langley in Hertfordshire. Her passions include 80s alternative rock music and to unwind she enjoys a game of backgammon and reading (in the bath).

Glossary

Definitions of some of the terms that crop up frequently throughout this book.

Call to action – An enticement, recommendation or request to follow a particular course of action, usually one that will result in a benefit of some kind (such as an uplift in sales or a better world).

Charisma – Charm.

Comfort zone – A situation where you feel safe.

Conscious mind – Feelings and thoughts within your awareness.

Meditation – Time spent in quiet thought.

Mindfulness – A state of non-judgemental awareness.

Mindset – Mental attitude.

Mojo – Power or talent.

Presence – State of complete awareness; ideal state of mind for public speaking.

Rapport – Your ability to understand and be understood by other people.

Re-frame – To put in a different context (more positively in the case of this book).

Self-esteem – How you feel about yourself.

Self-talk – Your thoughts or 'internal dialogue' pertaining to your own abilities. Self-talk can be positive or negative.

Unconscious mind – Feelings and thoughts outside your awareness.

Visualisation – The creation of mental images.

Preface

Sometimes, when I'm sitting on yet another train or squeezed onto another plane trying to work on my presentation I wonder why it is that we go to so much effort to get together with other people just so a few of us can talk out loud in front of an audience.

In a world of Skype chats, Google Hangouts and videoconferences, Whatsapp messages and email exchanges, Tweets and Facebook status updates we still feel the need to come together and talk to each other, choosing to share spaces and experiences.

I know the answer, of course, and that's why you'll find me in Dundee, Dublin, Delhi and Delaware giving talks at conferences, chairing panel sessions or offering my contribution to seminars and symposia.

Sharing the same space is a core part of being human, and no technical innovations we may come up with in the future will stop us wanting to be with other people: we are social animals, living in the world of atoms not the world of bits. We simply work better with other people around us, even laptop warriors like me who spend a lot of time moving around and make the best use they can of technologies that connect us to colleagues, friends and family.

This tells us something deep about the world and our place in it, but it also means that however much you may try to avoid them, there are always going to be meetings, conferences, events, seminars, presentations and talks.

And that means that there will always be those moments when someone – you – has to stand up in front of other people and share their thoughts, make a pitch, explain a project or defend their ideas.

If you hate that thought, then this book is for you.

If you've had a bad experience, or managed to avoid being thrust into the spotlight, or even if you have made many presentations but always felt terrified at the prospect and unhappy with your delivery, then the advice you'll find here can help you find the confidence you need to stand up and speak without (too much) fear and give a great performance.

This isn't just a book to skim read and put back on the shelf but a practical guide with many simple exercises that will, if you try them, significantly change the way you think about your public speaking performance. It will change the way you view yourself and the way you prepare for and deliver every presentation, from a short thank you at the end of a birthday dinner to the career-making pitch to your next boss or the future investors in your world-changing startup.

It tells you the things you really need to know, especially when it comes to the hard, tedious stuff like rehearsing, and it doesn't pull any punches:

Most people are not committed to doing what it takes to ensure their performance is great. Most people prefer to not think about their performance until the night before they are due to do it. Most people think rehearsals are boring and unnecessary. Most people are destined to be mediocre public speakers!

That one spoke to me, because I know that sometimes I don't do the preparation I need, preferring to 'wing it' so I can spend more time on Twitter.

This inspiring book also manages to crystallise the core lessons in an unforgettable way: if I ever get a tattoo, I could do much worse than use one of Julie's lessons – of which my favourite is probably:

Bring the loveliest version of yourself to the stage

Even if you're a regular and fairly confident speaker, you'll find a lot of sound advice. For example, reading Julie's book made me realise that I always prepare too much material, confident that I can edit on the fly if I have to. I could save myself some work and reduce the stress I feel when the person in front of me overruns if I took her advice and prepared ten per cent less than I think I will need.

So next time you see me give a talk, come up afterwards and ask me if I took my good friend's advice!

BILL THOMPSON, BBC WORLD SERVICE

About Bill

Bill Thompson has been working in, on and around the Internet since 1984 and spends his time considering the ways digital technologies are changing our world. A well-known technology journalist and public speaker, he gives thirty or forty talks a year on a wide range of topics.

He appears weekly on Click on BBC World Service radio, writes a column for Focus magazine and advises a range of arts and cultural organisations on their digital

strategies. He is a member of the boards of Writers'
Centre Norwich, Britten Sinfonia and The Collections
Trust, and was formerly a Trustee of the Cambridge Film
Trust. He manages the Working for an MP website at
w4mp.org

Introduction

> "It is not selfish to be happy.
> It is your highest purpose.
> Your joy is the greatest
> contribution you can make
> to life on the planet."
>
> — NICK WILLIAMS —

There are far too many books about public speaking fear. With this book, I hope to re-dress the balance.

I have been a public speaker for nearly half of my life.

Like most people, I was a reluctant public speaker at first. I could do it, but it was usually a case of endurance rather than enjoyment.

All of that changed in the mid-1990s, when I began work as a disability rights campaigner for the Royal National Institute of Blind People in London. I was tasked with creating a campaign to convince web designers, businesses and the Government to make changes to their websites so that disabled people would find them easier to use.

Never one to follow the herd (or do what I'm told) I privately questioned my esteemed colleagues' preference for letter-writing and ministerial meetings. It struck me that to make a real difference you needed to find ways to get the public behind you.

So I embarked on a modest crusade to create a grassroots movement, through which I hoped to inspire people who were sympathetic to the cause to join me. I don't think I wrote a single letter in the seven years that I worked on that campaign. I'd found a much more dangerous weapon to use in my fight against injustice. That weapon of 'mass discussion' was public speaking.

I deserted my desk and hit the road, with my feet in my black leather boots and my suitcase-on-wheels by my side, banging the drum for disability rights wherever I went. I built a loyal following of supporters who turned out to see me speak in village halls, conference centres and university lecture theatres across the land. Together, we created a groundswell that led to real change in the lives of many disabled people, the effects of which are still enjoyed today.

Public speaking touches people in a way that only public speaking can. If you want to create social change then public speaking will be one of the most powerful weapons in your armoury. If your aim is to generate sales leads or to demonstrate thought leadership within your industry, public speaking is a memorable and cost-effective way to reach potential customers en masse with power and passion.

Not every talk can go well, and I've experienced my fair share of disappointment on the road. So how, as I dragged my tired feet and my little suitcase-on wheels through the wind and the rain after another dismally low turn-out in a corner of England I had never previously heard of did I maintain the resolve to keep on putting myself through it? The answer is plain: there is no greater feeling than when someone who has heard me speak on such an occasion later informs me that it was I who inspired them to make positive changes in the world.

It feels great to help people in a meaningful and enduring way by doing something that also brings me genuine enjoyment. I believe everyone can get pleasure from public speaking. You just need to know how it's done and this book will give you all the help you need.

Within these pages you will come across plenty of clear and clever advice, such as why it's important to be a diva and how thinking of nothing will help you to come up with brilliant ideas for your presentations. I even tell you how to deal with a badly behaved audience (without losing your temper).

You can't learn public speaking from a book so I've created fifty short videos to accompany the fifty imaginative exercises. How great is that?

I hope the ideas on the pages that follow will ignite a fire inside you. It's my mission to create public speaking powerhouses in all of us, so follow me and join my revolution! Write to me at Julie@publicspeakingmojo.co.uk – I'd love to know what you think of the book.

To paraphrase Henry Ford, whether you believe you're a great public speaker or not you're right. It's time to start believing.

JULIE HOWELL, ABBOTS LANGLEY, HERTFORDSHIRE, ENGLAND, SPRING 2014

Chapter One

Mojo, where art thou?

> # "To avoid criticism, do nothing, say nothing and be nothing."
>
> — ELBERT HUBBARD —

The problem is not what you think it is

Most people are apprehensive the first time they speak in public. So it must have come as a huge relief when your first experience wasn't nearly as bad as you had imagined it would be. The ground didn't swallow you up. There were no 'wardrobe malfunctions'. To everyone's surprise, the video embedded in your presentation played right on cue (and as all seasoned public speakers know, while the video will play in rehearsals 100% of the time, when it comes to the live presentation the odds are slashed to 50/50).

With increased confidence you speak again and for a second time and then a third your presentation is smooth sailing. 'I'm a naturally gifted public speaker!' you think, and you are not the only one thinking it. People who see your presentations go out of their way to tell you how much they have enjoyed them.

Then one sunny day something BAD happens.

It is as though the 'magic' that has made you a great public speaker has suddenly and without any warning worn off.

Words stick in your throat, your voice sounds like it belongs to someone else and a woman in the fourth row with the piercing blue eyes who reminds you of your mother shoots disapproving looks your way every time you make eye contact with her.

By the time the horrendous ordeal is over you feel hopelessly deflated. Nothing makes any sense. Your preparation (such as it was) was no different to last time. If anything, your slides were a bit flashier. And you were definitely wearing your lucky pants (because just before you walked on stage one of your colleagues pointed out that your zip was undone). You had brushed *and* flossed your teeth. Yet nothing about this presentation felt good.

Where did your mojo go?

Brace yourself because I'm about to deliver a shock.

Remember those first few occasions when everything went well and people told you what a natural you are at public speaking? We more experienced public speakers have a name for this phenomenon. It's called 'a run of beginner's luck'.

You are not a natural born public speaker

No one is born a 'naturally talented' public speaker.

It's true, I'm afraid. There is no natural talent involved. Great public speaking is a result of practice, experience and commitment (stay with me, the book gets better).

Great public speakers succeed every time because they commit themselves to mastering the techniques of great public speaking. They put in the effort that is required to become a great speaker and are never complacent about their skills.

And this is fantastic news for you.

You haven't *lost* your ability to be a great public speaker. You are just inexperienced. Put the right type of effort in and you will get your public speaking mojo back forever. That's a promise.

Leaving it to chance

You have made one simple, classic mistake. You have left your success to chance.

You could make another presentation tomorrow and chances are it will be great. The laws of probability may work in your favour one more time. But *why* leave it to chance? Wouldn't you like to be certain that you will give a fantastic presentation every time? Wouldn't it be great to get rid of presentation anxiety forever? With the right kind of practice you can.

This is the main difference between you and successful public speakers. In those moments before stepping on stage successful speakers *know* they are about to give the best performance possible. You, on the other hand, *hope* you are about to give the best performance possible. Hope has no place on the public speaking platform. Hope is as likely to guarantee failure and disappointment as success. Hope is the opposite of *knowing*. Knowing will enable you to give your very best performance every single time.

I know I will give my very best performance every time I speak in public. Would you like to know my secrets? Then keep reading because I wrote this book especially for you.

The key

You won't be surprised when I tell you the key to 'knowing' is practice. However, it is a very specific kind of practice, a kind you probably haven't come across before. It doesn't involve memorising your presentation and it doesn't require any expensive re-training. In this book, I will tell you how to use tools you already have to develop a public speaking skillset that will guarantee you will give the presentation you intended to give every time.

Public speaking is a skillset

Public speaking performance is not the same as acting; it is more difficult but also more rewarding. Unlike an actor, you do not work from a script and your sole responsibility is not to entertain – that would be easier! Public speaking is a set of skills and it will take time and commitment on your part to master them all.

Don't wait until there is an emergency

An unpleasant public speaking experience will put a dent in your pride. You may feel embarrassed. Your ego may take a nasty knock. You will probably want to put as much distance between yourself and the bad experience as you can. Alas, you can try to run from embarrassment but you cannot hide from it. You know that one day you will have to get back on that stage and put yourself through the turmoil all over again. When you are least prepared for it, a friend will ask you to speak at his wedding, your boss will ask you to speak in her absence, or, worse still, you will be asked, at very short notice, to speak at the funeral of a close friend.

An emergency is the worst time to try to get your public speaking mojo back. Start to take steps in the right direction now so that when you are asked to speak (and in the case of a friend's funeral you may decide you really do *want* to speak) you will be confident that you will do your very best. Grab the bull by the horns today. Your future self will thank you for it.

(If you *are* in a public speaking emergency right now, skip forward to Chapter 16 where I list some fixes that will help you right away.)

It's a tragedy

It is little short of tragic when someone as knowledgeable and experienced as you loses the desire to speak in public. This waste of talent concerns me so much that it inspired me to write this book packed with useful advice and techniques to help you get your public speaking mojo back forever.

Far too many professional people like you lose faith in their public speaking abilities prematurely because of one or two bad experiences. But remember, any skill takes time to master. When you were very small you fell down many times in an effort to learn how to walk. Walking is a skill that must be learned. As a baby you persevered until you could walk. Every time you fell you got back up again, so strong was your desire for independence. It is time for you to apply the same amount of determination to acquiring the skills of public speaking.

Can we make an agreement?

The advice in this book will help you to understand how to give a really great talk to any audience in any circumstance at any time. You will learn how to handle challenging situations. You will appreciate why the right kind of preparation and the right kind of practice are so important. Let's make a commitment to one another to do the things you need to do to become a confident and effective public speaker. I will provide the information and fifty very helpful exercises that you can easily practise on your own. You will commit to working through the exercises at whatever pace suits you.

Just like a successful athlete, you are committing yourself to doing all the things that will ensure you always give a great performance. After all, the people in your audience deserve your very best.

Together we will get your public speaking mojo back for good.

Not for people with social anxiety

This book is not intended to help you to overcome social anxiety or a phobia of speaking in public. If you think this is you then you may find a cognitive behavioural therapist who specialises in social anxiety disorder helpful. You will find a list of registered UK cognitive behavioural therapists on the British Psychological Society website at www.BPS.org.uk. I do not pretend to be something I am not. If you need the kind of help only a qualified therapist can provide then please seek one out.

Ready to work?

No book will restore your public speaking mojo for you. The only way to get your public speaking mojo back is through work and commitment, but I am with you every step of the way.

Give it a go!

Throughout this book I will help you to re-discover your mojo by encouraging you to 'Give it a go!'. There are fifty exercises in this book designed to help you take practical steps to increase your public speaking confidence.

Don't worry, you don't have to try all fifty! Depending on your personal learning style some of the exercises will suit you, others will not. Take your time, it is not a test. Try a couple of exercises each week. Think of Mo Farrah, not Usain Bolt. This is the ten thousand metres, not a sprint!

To help you out even further I've created a video for every exercise that explains in greater detail exactly what you need to do. Each video has subtitles. Not only does this mean the exercises are fully accessible to deaf and hard-of-hearing people, if you are reading this book on a train or bus and don't have your headphones with you, you can still watch and understand the videos without any sound.

You will find the videos online at www.publicspeakingmojo.co.uk in the password-protected area of the site. The password is **h3110m0j0**

Chapter Two

You are not alone (everyone does it!)

> ## "What? You too? I thought I was the only one."
>
> — C.S. LEWIS —

I really do know how you feel

Every new client I see believes they are the only person in the world who struggles with public speaking in the way that they do. It doesn't seem to matter how old they are or the level of seniority they hold within their company. People from all walks of life worry about public speaking and worry that they worry about it.

It seems the more confident and successful a person is the more determined they are to hide their discomfort about public speaking. It is as if you feel that you don't have the right to ask for help because the world should believe that you are brilliant at everything and have no 'weaknesses'. After all, so many successful business people are also wonderful speakers. They must have a natural gift! It is embarrassing to admit that you find public speaking difficult. Even if you decide that you need some help, getting in touch with a public speaking coach is a daunting step.

What happened in the past

When I meet a client for the first time he or she usually wants to spend the first fifty-nine minutes of our sixty-minute session talking about the past. More specifically he or she wants to talk about bad things that have happened in the past, such as the negative feedback he or she received after giving a presentation to the board or what his or her mother said about his or her poor posture or mumbling voice. New clients assume that as a successful speaking coach I must want to analyse every one of his or her 'failings' so that I can provide advice how to correct whatever I diagnose is 'wrong'.

What happened to you in the past is of no interest to me. Ideas you may have about why you are not a good public speaker amount to little more than emotional baggage in my eyes. Clients visibly relax when I reassure them that, as I wasn't present at any of their past talks, I cannot vouch for the reliability of the negative feedback they have received. What I *would* like to do, however, is use our sixty precious minutes to talk about the kind of public speaker they would like to be.

When you imagine yourself as a successful speaker, what do you see? How does thinking about yourself as a successful speaker make you feel? If you knew you were a successful speaker how would it change your attitude towards public speaking? I find your answers to these questions far more interesting than a list of reasons why you don't like yourself very much. When I know where you want to be we can start working on a plan to get you there.

A prayer for what you don't want

This is a lovely phrase that may resonate with you: a worry is a prayer for what you don't want.

Do you find the more you worry about something the bigger the problem seems to get? Worries about the past are baggage. Worries about the future are baggage. Baggage doesn't belong on stage so we won't let baggage of any kind concern us. I could indulge you in your worries about what you or someone else thinks has been 'wrong' with your past presentations but how would doing so help you to move forward? Worrying keeps you stuck in a negative state of mind.

What follows is the first exercise I set for delegates of my 'Communicate with Confidence' workshops. It's designed to get you thinking about what is really true about your ability to be a great public speaker. Don't let its simplicity fool you. Take this opportunity to work through the exercise. The results may surprise you. Your journey to getting your public speaking mojo back starts here.

GIVE IT A GO! 1
Does it matter?

Make a list of every negative thought that you have about yourself as a public speaker. Dig deep and list as many as you can.

Add to this list every negative piece of feedback that anyone who has heard you speak has ever given you.

When you have made your list read through it carefully and ask yourself this question: "What if none of these things matter?"

Some of the items on your list may be true. Some may only be true in certain circumstances. Others may only be true when a certain person is saying them. Some may not be true at all.

Now ask yourself these questions:

'What if, true or false, not one of the statements on my list matters at all?'

'What would happen if I was to agree that none of these statements matter?'

'What would happen if I was to agree to not give these statements any further thought?'

Now delete or draw a line through every item on your list one at a time. As you do so, read the item aloud followed by "This does not matter".

When you have scored through every item on your list delete or discard it. What happened in the past is not needed any more.

Remember to watch the video at www.publicspeakingmojo.co.uk

Let's start afresh

Holding on to other people's negative feedback won't help you get your public speaking mojo back. Criticism can hurt and can be difficult to forget, even when the criticism was intended to be 'constructive'. When you move away from negative comments you take very positive steps towards being the kind of speaker you really want to be and the kind of speaker you are capable of being.

Chapter Three

Re-frame your 'bad' experience

> ## "Have no fear of perfection – you'll never reach it."
>
> — SALVADOR DALI —

Stop expecting perfection

Are you your own worst critic, quick to find fault with yourself, slow to accept a compliment from another person? I suspect most people are. However, there is one criticism I *would* like to level at you: when it comes to the quality of your public speaking the standard you set for yourself is too high and your unreasonable expectations are likely to be harming your performance.

When you get the feeling that your presentation isn't going as well as you had hoped it would you begin to give off verbal and non-verbal signals that are very obvious to the people in your audience, such as tutting, sighing, apologising and looking unhappy (slumped shoulders, looking at the ground more, smiling less). We have all watched someone 'die' on stage, and as audience members we have 'died' along with them. If you feel disappointed with yourself, and show visible or audible signs of your disappointment, the people in your audience will begin to feel disappointed too. It's surprisingly easy to spread a bad feeling around a room.

Why spread a bad feeling and spoil everyone else's day? As the speaker, it is your responsibility to set a reasonable expectation with yourself and to commit to achieving that level of performance. People who are disappointed with themselves are not pleasant to watch. No one comes to a conference hoping to feel bad!

You may want to be as great an orator as Steve Jobs or Eleanor Roosevelt, but you are not Steve Jobs or Eleanor Roosevelt. You are you, and you are perfectly good enough. Your audience wants to hear from you, and deserves to hear the best of you. While it is important to work on becoming the best that you can be, you don't help your audience when you set a standard for yourself that you rarely or never achieve.

Many factors

There are many factors that can affect a live presentation that cannot be predicted and are beyond your control. In this regard all speakers are equal!

Be realistic. No matter how well you prepare sometimes things will go wrong. It is how you respond in a 'crisis' that matters. If you expect everything to go your way during every presentation you will almost always leave the stage feeling disappointed and frustrated. Before too long your disappointment will become cynicism and that cynicism will feed the 'negative self-talk' in your head that is telling you that you are not and will never be a good enough public speaker (more about negative self-talk in Chapter 5).

Rather than seek perfection, commit yourself to putting your audience's needs at the heart of every presentation you give. Approach your presentations with patience, compassion, understanding and complete focus on the needs of the people in your audience and you will always come out on top, not matter what happens around you. If your audience is happy (they will be if their needs, objectives and expectations are met) then you are doing a great job.

Many responsibilities

A public speaker is never only a public speaker. You are also your own stage manager with responsibilities that reach far beyond keeping to time and remembering to say your key points. You are working with a live audience and you have many responsibilities to them that include helping them to learn something new and inspiring them to respond to your 'calls to action', as well as making sure they are comfortable and can see and hear you (more about your many responsibilities in Chapter 10).

Your audience is more forgiving than you are

The people in your audience don't mind the odd mishap. Truly, they just don't care. They probably didn't even notice that something went wrong. They are far too interested in what you have to say to let every small interruption frustrate them.

When something goes awry, pause and be aware of what is happening in the room around you. This skill of complete and non-judgemental awareness is called 'presence'. It is one of the most important skills you need to master to be a great public speaker (more about presence in Chapter 11).

So something 'bad' happened during one of your presentations...

When something goes spectacularly wrong during one of your presentations you, being a perfectly sensible and rational person, may decide that you are never going to speak in public again. One humiliating experience is more than enough for most people.

Would it surprise you to know that I feel this way occasionally too? I suspect every public speaker does, even the most experienced ones. Yet we continue to put ourselves through it because, even though there have been occasions when things have not gone the way we intended, when a presentation does goes well there is little else in our professional lives that bring us so much pleasure or a deeper sense of accomplishment and connection to our purpose.

I still make mistakes all the time

I have been a public speaker for twenty years. Yet I still make the odd mistake, because I'm human. Very recently, I turned up to a make a presentation having made a big fuss with the organiser of the event about having access to a projector. So imagine the shame and humiliation I felt when I popped my memory stick into the laptop only to discover that I'd forgotten to copy my presentation onto it. The shame!

So what did I do? I told the audience that I had decided I would rather talk *to* them rather than *at* them and gave the presentation that I'd rehearsed without any visual aids at all. No one noticed my mistake and I lived to present another day.

An opportunity in disguise

In Chapter 2 I explained that I never ask my clients to dwell on past disappointments. However, I would like to help you to 're-frame' them. Is there really such a thing as a 'bad experience' or is there any chance that what happened to you was an opportunity in disguise?

Over the past twenty years a lot of unwelcome and unanticipated things have happened during my presentations, from equipment failure to a siege, twice (Think I'm joking? See Chapter 4!). However, none of these so-called 'negative' experiences has ended my career as a speaker.

It may be a cliché, but disappointments and disasters are almost always learning opportunities. A disaster is only truly a disaster if nothing is learned from it. If catastrophe does pay you a visit, look for what can be learned and move on. If you keep learning you are always moving forward towards your goal of being the best speaker you can be.

It is helpful to greet every problem as a learning experience but this only works if you are convinced that there is something to be learned. It is time to develop a mindset whereby you really believe that you have as much to learn each time you speak in public as the people in your audiences do.

One size does not fit all

Public speaking should never be done on 'auto pilot' and your presentations are never 'one size fits all'. Every presentation you give should be as unique as the audience you are speaking to. I'm not referring to the content so much as the manner in which you deliver your presentation, which should always be responsive to the unspoken signals that you receive from the people in your audience. This requires the skills of awareness and presence as well as tenacity, patience, compassion and flexibility.

Your development as a public speaker is organic. It happens while you are making a presentation. It is not a competency you can learn from books alone. It is a set of skills that can only develop when you put yourself in front of audience after audience in any setting you can think of (and many you can't imagine!).

We're all human

The people in your audience are human beings and they are intelligent and wise. They understand that the person on stage is also human. What's more, this is exactly why they have chosen to come to hear you speak. If they were satisfied by reading books or watching YouTube videos they would not have made the effort to come and watch you live and in person. An audience of any size is a compliment and the people in your audience understand what it is to be human. In almost all cases they will forgive a mistake or two.

Embrace your mistakes because in their own funny ways they are a signal to the people in your audience that you are a fallible human being, just like them. As a wise manager once said to me when I was cross with myself for making a mistake, 'It's good to know you make mistakes. I was starting to think you were a robot.'

The people in your audience are not looking for perfection. What they want more than anything is to learn something from you that they can apply in their own lives.

Helping people feels good

It is so important to challenge negative beliefs about yourself when they interfere with your ability to help other people. 'Challenge' should not mean becoming angry with yourself for feeling the way that you do. 'Challenge' simply means asking yourself 'is this negative belief that I have about myself actually true?'

When you make a decision to believe that you can help people through public speaking you unlock the door to feelings of pleasure and satisfaction about yourself as a speaker. Doesn't it feel great when you tell someone something that helps them to do their job better? Sharing your knowledge and expertise is a fast route to happiness for you and for the people you are speaking to.

Whether it's gossip, trivia or a fact that can directly or indirectly save a life the knowledge that you have contributed in some way to the prosperity of another person feels really good. When speaking to a business audience, what you share may translate into profits and jobs. That's an incredible impact to have on the world. Enjoy how this feels. When you speak to a group of people you have the opportunity to reproduce this wonderful feeling many times over.

Audiences rarely behave the way you expect them to

In twenty years of public speaking I have learned this fundamental fact about audiences: they are unpredictable. I have seen many good presenters come unstuck when they have expected the people in their audience to respond in a certain way, such as laugh in a particular place in their presentation. (British stand-up comedian Stewart Lee makes many observations about audience behaviour that public speakers will find familiar and very amusing.)

Unless you plant people in the audience with strict instructions on how to behave you have no way of knowing how they will react. When putting your presentation together be sure that you are not relying on the audience to react in a specific way for the presentation to succeed.

You're not a TED talker (yet)

You may have watched videos on the internet of people speaking at the famous TED conferences around the world (if you aren't familiar with TED I highly recommend you take a look at www.TED.com).

Watch any 'TED Talk' and notice how the people in the audience behave at the close of each talk. In almost every case the speaker receives either a standing ovation or, at the very least, rapturous applause. Without meaning to cause offence to any of the fantastic TED speakers, it appears the TED audience reacts warmly to everyone they listen to. They do, but with good reason.

TED events have an atmosphere particular to TED where the people in the audience conform to a convention that includes applauding wildly at the end of every talk. There is nothing at all wrong with this except that it may have given you a false expectation about how the people in your own audiences are likely to behave.

No one has ever stood and applauded at the end of one of my presentations. That is not to say I haven't been appreciated! The fact is it is rare to receive a standing ovation or rapturous applause at many conferences outside TED. Your audience will politely applaud but unless they are trying to leave the room they will probably stay seated. Don't take this as a sign that they are unhappy. Standing ovations are rare. If you get one, fantastic! If you don't, that's okay too.

What your audience is really thinking

Staying with TED for a moment, watch any TED talk and notice the expressions on the faces of the people in the audience when the cameras pan around the venue. What you will see are expressions of wonderment and joy. Everyone looks fully engrossed in what the speaker is saying. Some may even appear to wipe a tear from their eye.

What you are seeing is the power of post-production. The shots of the people in the audience have been carefully selected and edited together. Naturally, the director will choose shots of people looking animated, moved or happy.

Don't feel discouraged if the people in your audiences seem less enthusiastic when you're talking. TED talk videos are designed to entertain. It would be more than a bit odd if a talk was cut with shots of the audience looking depressed and despondent (which, take it from me, is how they tend to look when they are concentrating!). If your audience looks less than delighted, don't take it to heart. It is what's going on inside their heads that matters and what they do with what they have learned from your presentation that counts.

Indulge them

There is a very simple explanation for why a presentation that felt funny or surprising when you performed it in your head might fail to stir a reaction from the people in your audience when you give the presentation for real. When an audience listens to a talk their concentration is repeatedly broken by at least three processes, none of which is within your control:

- They are thinking about what you are saying and how they might apply it in their own lives

- They are taking notes

- They are Tweeting (Twitter can be a blessing or a curse)

You want your audience to do all of these things.

However, when the people in your audience are thinking, note-taking or Tweeting, their focus (their attention) is temporarily directed towards what they are doing and not towards what you are saying. This means they may miss your jokes, your key points or your big moments of revelation. This is why you might hear silence when where you may reasonably have expected laughter or gasps.

The people in your audience might also fail to react unless you deliver your presentation with power and charisma (in Chapter 11 I take a deeper look at how you can deliver a powerful, memorable, high impact performance).

If it is important to the flow of your presentation that your audience reacts in a certain way at a certain time then you must direct them and take responsibility for ensuring it happens.

↯ Use a dramatic pause to bring their attention back to you

↯ Use gesture and tone to make them aware that you are saying something important

↯ If you want to be absolutely sure they have heard your key messages, repeat them and look for signs that most of them have heard you (such as facial expressions, head movements or sudden, frantic note-taking!).

Re-frame your 'bad' experiences

When presentations go according to plan what do you learn? Where is the opportunity for growth? I would rather endure the temporary discomfort of a presentation going wrong than the relative comfort of a presentation going right because problems are often great learning experiences in disguise.

It's time to re-frame your 'bad' experiences. All contain hidden gifts that will help you to develop, improve and grow. Let go of the desire to get it 'right' all the time and embrace the greater gifts of learning and development.

The audience really is on your side

It is easy to get caught up in your own feelings of disappointment and frustration when your presentation doesn't go to plan. But ask yourself this: were the people in the audience let down in any way or is it only you that is unhappy? We are all our own harshest critics. In your haste to admonish yourself do you forget the real reason why you speak on your subject?

GIVE IT A GO! 2
How they describe me

Put down this book for a few minutes and think about the bad experience that made you decide that public speaking wasn't for you. Recall how you felt on that day, on that stage, in front of those people.

After a few minutes spent remembering as much as you can about that occasion switch your focus to the moment when you decided that everything had gone irreversibly wrong. Note how you felt at that time, how you have felt about that moment ever since, how you have described that moment to people who weren't there and how you feel about it now. Do not think about 'what ifs' or about where to put the blame. Just observe your own thoughts and feelings.

Now write a list of adjectives that describe those thoughts, feelings and emotions. The list can be as long as you like.

When you have finished making your list, consider each word that you have written and ask yourself 'Are these really the words that people who admire me and look to me for knowledge and inspiration would choose to describe me?'

Delete any words that they would **not** use to describe you. You will not need those any more. Of the words that remain ask yourself, 'Do I need to believe this about myself?' and 'What will my life be like if I dismiss these words as easily as I dismissed the others?'

While these words may represent feelings or emotions that felt very real at the time, what happens if you choose to believe that they are neither useful nor relevant to you now? Can you now delete all the words on your list? If any remain, do you know why you are choosing to believe them?

Remember to watch the video at www.publicspeakingmojo.co.uk

Chapter Four

When bad things happen to good speakers

> ## "Things do not happen. Things are made to happen."
>
> — JOHN F. KENNEDY —

Bad things happen for a reason

Bad things usually happen because you aren't fully prepared. However, a little bit of bad fortune can be a golden opportunity to impress the people in your audience if you handle the catastrophe with poise and charm.

Here is a list of five things that can go wrong during a presentation and some clever ideas on how you can emerge from a crisis victorious.

1. Too few people have turned up

It can be soul-destroying when you've been told to expect two hundred people for your presentation and only three turn up (as has happened to me on more than one occasion). Of course you feel despondent. A big audience brings with it so much energy and that energy can fuel your performance. But cheer up. Who knows what these three souls might do with what you tell them that the absent one hundred and ninety-seven could not. Always treat your audience, however small, as though they are the most important audience you will ever speak to.

GIVE IT A GO! 3
It only takes one person to change the world

The next time you experience a 'disappointing turnout' (to use the popular euphemism for poor marketing) remind yourself that it only takes one person to change the world.

Imagine that person could be one of the people sitting before you.

Give your presentation everything you've got. Lavish the audience with attention.

Make it the greatest presentation of your career (and encourage them to tell everyone they know about it!).

Remember to watch the video at www.publicspeakingmojo.co.uk

Those precious few who have turned out to hear you speak have chosen you over a hundred other choices they could have taken that day. Reward them for their excellent taste with a presentation they'll remember for all the right reasons. Who knows, they may become your best advocates and greatest allies.

If someone in your modest audience remarks that the turnout is poor respond positively. Assure them that you are just as excited about presenting your ideas to them as you would be to an audience of three thousand!

And if no one turns up, give your presentation anyway! Treat it as a further opportunity to rehearse. Never let an opportunity for practice pass you by. You never know, there may be latecomers who will be very pleased that you didn't allow their tardiness to deter you from going ahead with your presentation.

2. Your presentation is repeatedly interrupted by external noise

If your efforts to provide the right environment for the people in your audience to see and hear your presentation clearly fall short, briefly acknowledge and apologise for the interruption or distraction, keep going, and make extra effort after your presentation to speak to people individually where possible.

This may sound like a lot of additional work given the problem may not have been your fault – and it is – but it will be well worth the effort. We speak to start relationships. Noise can be a blessing in disguise if it results in more one-to-one conversations with people who are truly interested in what you have to say.

3. Your audience is indifferent to you

It is not for you to dictate how people in the audience should react to your presentation. If they laugh at the parts you intend to be funny, great! But it is equally likely that they won't react at all.

Remember that your presentation is a channel for your message and not a platform for your ego. Your goal is not to be approved of or appreciated. Your goal is to inform and influence to the best of your ability. This should be your focus: ensuring that your message is received loud and clear. If the people in your audience appear unmoved keep going. Their apparent indifference may belie a great deal of brain activity below the surface!

4. Your technology isn't doing what it is supposed to be doing

There is no excuse for allowing technology to upstage you. Always have a back-up plan so that you can continue without the people in your audience noticing there has been a glitch (and you should resist the urge to announce the glitch!).

Some of my most memorable and enjoyable performances have happened when my technology has failed completely. What a fantastic opportunity to impress the people in your audience by showing them how cool you are in an apparent crisis. If you're not yet comfortable with the idea of presenting without slides then make sure you don't rely on one piece of technology for your presentation to work. Always have a 'plan b' (a second copy of your presentation, an extra laptop on standby, screen grabs in case the Wi-Fi should stop working).

5. You are over-running because your timeslot has been reduced

Timeslot reduction is a real and present danger. It is usually the fault of the speaker before you or a failure on the part of the Chairperson to keep the conference running to time. Even though it is not your fault that your timeslot has been reduced you must keep within the revised time (no matter how much it irks you!). If you don't, you are only adding to the problem of a poorly-run event when you could be part of the solution.

The following, very simple tip has helped me on many occasions. Always plan to speak for around fifteen percent fewer minutes than requested. Never prepare twenty minutes of material if your presentation slot is twenty minutes long. Prepare around fifteen minutes of material instead. Then, if you are required to speak for less time than you originally expected, you won't be the one caught out.

Preparing less material than you need is standard good practice. Interruptions can always eat into your time but over-running is very bad form indeed. It is better to finish your presentation early than out-stay your welcome (a lesson, I confess, that took me some years to grasp).

It is uncomfortable to watch a speaker getting into a flap because he or she is over-running and trying to find a way to end his or her talk prematurely yet on a powerful note. Let other speakers over-run and make sure you keep to time even if it means forfeiting some of your excellent content. It is better to leave the people in your audience wanting more than to leave them feeling annoyed because you have made them late home.

GIVE IT A GO! 4
Judging yourself

Think about the last time you came away from a presentation feeling disappointed with yourself because it did not go the way you had hoped it would.

Observe your thoughts and feelings about this experience.

Are they true or are you judging yourself too harshly?

Is it possible that the people in the audience may have really loved your presentation despite its faults?

Are you allowing your ego, the part of you that wants to be successful all the time, blind you to the needs of the people you are talking to?

Remember to watch the video at www.publicspeakingmojo.co.uk

The difficult 'in-house' audience

The most challenging audience tends to be the one comprised of people who know each other very well, for example, your own colleagues or people in another company.

If you are asked to speak at another company's board meeting, for instance, be prepared for members of the group to 'misbehave' while you are speaking, even though you are an invited guest!

Behaviour that may include talking amongst themselves, laughing with one another at a private joke, checking emails, fidgeting or doodling may feel like an obvious and intentional display of disrespect towards you. However, they may be completely unaware that they are doing any of these things or the impact that their behaviour is having on you. So why do they do it?

Their behaviour is unlikely to be a reflection on your performance. Instead, it is merely their unconscious attempt to remain dominant in their own domain. Look out for senior managers who sit leaning back, their hands clasped behind their heads. What do you think they are unconsciously doing? It is simple: they are making themselves appear bigger in an attempt to assert their dominance. Some will stand up and walk around the room, others with tap away at their status symbol smartphones.

Rather than take offence or let their behaviour distract you expect them to behave this way and understand why they do it. It is unlikely to be personal. They are simply letting you that you are the guest and they are in charge!

'Play harder'

Having been to many rock concerts where people in the audience haven't even bothered to look towards the stage when the band is playing I wondered how rock musicians feel when their audience is lairy, uninterested or simply unappreciative. I asked a musician who plays bass in a popular rock band what she does when people in her audiences behave in a disrespectful or uninterested manner. Her reply surprised me: 'I play harder', she said.

Rather than interrupt the show to berate badly behaved audience members musicians put even greater effort into playing as well as they possibly can. I like this response very much and wondered what it means for us speakers. How can we 'play harder'? Should we shout, glare or stomp around the stage waving our arms until we have everyone's attention (clearly, this is never appropriate behaviour!)?

We can 'play harder' by becoming more engaging. Even the grumpiest audience members will take notice when a speaker has true passion for a subject.

Just as a musician might 'turn up' the level of their performance, we can turn our 'volume' up to eleven. Give your audience everything you've got. Those who were already attentive will appreciate your efforts and those who weren't might just get the message that something worthy of their attention is happening on the stage.

Recovery from a good presentation gone bad

When I was less experienced and if my presentation failed to live up to my very high expectations I wouldn't handle it very well. "I am never doing this again! I'm no good at it! No one listens to me!" I would whine.

On one such occasion a fellow speaker took me aside, and said, "Don't give up. If things haven't gone your way and you're feeling fed up, talk to someone about it."

He was so right. His words have stayed with me and led me to develop a very important aspect of my public speaking performance that helps me to move out of my over-the-top, over-confident, turned-up-to-eleven public speaking persona back into a state of mind that is more appropriate for civilian life. I call it my 'post-speaking routine'.

Your post-speaking routine

When you leave the stage you will probably be in a state of emotional arousal. It is not a good idea to stay in this highly aroused state for too long. The version of you that works so well on stage is likely to be a little too overwhelming for normal conversation. Take care of yourself after your presentation by establishing a post-speaking routine to help you to relax.

Your routine can include whatever you want it to. What matters is that you make sure you do something you enjoy that gently returns your mind to a calmer state.

↝ Meet with friends

↝ Read a book or watch a TV programme that you enjoy

↝ Meditate

↝ Have a relaxing bath

Things to avoid might include stimulants (such as caffeine) that prolong your state of arousal.

Bringing yourself back down to earth gently is an important aspect of your own self-care. Please take it just as seriously as all other aspects of your public speaking routine.

One speaker's disaster is this speaker's triumph

Some of my most problem-strewn presentations have also been my greatest public speaking triumphs because only when I've truly been tested have I shown the world just how brightly I can shine. As you will discover in the chapters that follow, it is all a case of mindset.

And if you should find yourself under siege...

I have spoken at hundreds of conferences over the past two decades. Statistically that allows for one or two to be in very strange circumstances. For instance, I have spoken at conferences under siege conditions twice in my life.

The first occasion was in Hampshire in around 2003, when a group of protesters smashed the glass doors of the Town Hall while I was speaking inside it. I'm slightly embarrassed to write about the subject of their disquiet so you'll just have to ask me what it was about when we meet. Needless to say, it was a local issue and my presence in the building on that day was pure coincidence.

The second occasion was on 7th July 2005. You may recognise this date instantly as the day of the London Bombings. I was speaking at a conference in London that day and once news of the nature of the emergency had filtered through to our hosts we (the panel of speakers and our audience members) were prohibited from leaving the building. I have never addressed an audience in such difficult circumstances. Some were clearly relieved by the distraction that my talk provided but most were preoccupied with their smartphones, desperate to hear that loved ones were safe.

In both situations I kept calm and carried on for what other option was there? In a crisis your audience looks to you for reassurance. Although you never expect a siege or even to deal with a fire alarm if it ever happens expect to take the lead in helping everyone present to maintain their composure. It has somehow become part of the speaker's special duty.

How to achieve happiness through public speaking

You will be a happy public speaker when you set your expectations correctly.

You will get a huge buzz from speaking when you know you have genuinely helped your audience to understand how they can apply what you have told them in their own lives. If this also leads to sales or new business leads, wonderful. If it leads to positive action in support of your campaign, fantastic. Your primary goal is to create a channel between you and the people in your audience through which communication can flow. When you get this right you will feel on top of the world (and so will they).

GIVE IT A GO! 5
Happy thoughts

Think for a few moments about the things in life that make you feel very happy. Notice how you feel when you think about these things.

When you feel happy your body produces hormones called endorphins that give you a feeling of exhilaration.

Next time you are preparing to go on stage, think about things that make you happy. When you do your brain will release endorphins into your body and you will begin your presentation feeling great.

Remember to watch the video at www.publicspeakingmojo.co.uk

Chapter Five

Why that great advice your family gave you isn't so great

> # "Be independent of the good opinion of other people"
>
> — ABRAHAM MASLOW —

Keep away from other people's good intentions

Your friends and family members have your best interests at heart. In an effort to help you get your public speaking mojo back someone who cares about you has probably offered to watch you rehearse your presentation and to give you some well-intended 'honest' feedback. If this happens to you politely, but firmly, decline because no good ever comes of it.

Not your audience

Your friends and family members are not the best people to give you public speaking advice because they are not your intended audience. They genuinely mean to help but their advice could do you more harm than good.

Bad advice

To show you what I mean, here are some examples of 'bad advice' that you may receive from your friends or family members:

1. "Just be yourself"

Your 'usual' self is not the person you should be when speaking to an audience. The public speaker in you is a type of leader with charisma and presence. To capture – and maintain – people's attention it is vital that you bring more energy to the stage than you would to an ordinary conversation. Be 'yourself' and you may be too casual and too quiet and lack the impact needed to properly engage the people in your audience with your message.

Many years ago, I received formal media training and the excellent advice I was given then has stayed with me to this day. I was told, "If your friends see you on TV and tell you that your behaviour was 'over-the-top' it's an indication that you're getting it right!"

When you speak in public you are a channel for a message. The version of yourself that you should bring to the stage is still you but with the 'volume' turned up to 'eleven'. By volume I don't just mean your sound, but everything – your posture, your gestures, your energy and your enthusiasm. Not turned up to 'twenty' (don't shout at or overwhelm the people in your audience), just to 'eleven' (one louder). Yourself, just even more so.

2. "Practise in front of a mirror"

If you catch sight of yourself in a mirror and don't like the 'turned up to eleven' version of yourself you will probably adjust your performance until you are happy with it.

Toning it down may make you feel more comfortable about what you see in the mirror but is not good for the people in your audience who need a slightly exaggerated performance to keep them engaged. The 'normal' you is too understated for the stage.

Avoid mirrors (and video cameras) because what matters is the power of your performance not how happy you are with the way you look.

3. "Practise in front of me"

You may have a childhood memory of practising lines from your school play in front of your mum. Or maybe you are now a parent forced to listen to verse after verse of that Andrew Lloyd Webber musical over and over again. This type of practice is fine because – for this occasion – you or your mum is representative of your audience.

In most public speaking situations, however, your friend, parent, child or spouse is not representative of your audience. Unless the person you are practising in front of is a speaking coach, a mentor or a member of your actual audience practising in front of people is very dangerous indeed.

Think about it. Feedback is highly subjective. Your well-meaning friend may encourage you to remove an element of your talk (perhaps because he or she thinks it is "too complicated") that would have given a great deal of valuable insight to the people in your actual audience.

Trust your own judgement. If you react to every piece of feedback what happens to your presentation? As the saying goes, a camel is a horse designed by a committee. Don't allow other people to input their ideas unless you are absolutely certain that their opinion is relevant.

If you are part of a team, for instance, if you are one of a group of people pitching an idea to a potential client, then it is important that you practise together. However, I still suggest that you also practise by yourself so that you can develop your contribution on your own before presenting it to your colleagues. You may be told that you need to change some elements of your contribution to fit in with everyone else but at least you will come to the first team rehearsal having prepared the structure of what you are going to say and how you are going to deliver it.

4. "Don't do that thing"

When you perform a presentation you are not 'yourself'. You are 'you', but turned up to 'eleven'. People who know you well may balk at this and encourage you to 'tone it down'. This is not the time to tone it down; it is the time to turn it up!

Friends and family might also advise you to eradicate any 'ticks' or mannerisms that they don't like. Your ticks and mannerisms are what make you 'you'. Instead of trying to get rid of your mannerisms begin to value them as expressions of your individuality. In Chapter 12, I will introduce to you a technique that will help you to become more aware of how you are performing that will help you to identify for yourself which mannerisms help your performance and which disturb your performance's flow.

GIVE IT A GO! 6
Bad advice

On this occasion **don't** give it a go!

The most effective way to practise your talk is on your own, with a timer using the 'mental rehearsal' technique that I describe in Chapter 12.

Remember to watch the video at www.publicspeakingmojo.co.uk

If friends and family members can't help, who can?

Everything you need to be a great public speaker is already inside you. Your main barrier right now is not your confidence (although you may think it is). Your main barrier is how you feel about yourself as a speaker. This is called your 'self-esteem'.

I use the word 'confidence' in the title of this book because books about confidence sell. The correct phrase in the context of your public speaking mojo is 'self-esteem'. Books and workshops about 'self-esteem' do not sell as well as books and workshops about 'confidence' because no one likes to think of themselves as being a person with low self-esteem. You may be thinking "Life's losers have low self-esteem, not people like me".

You already have high confidence

If you didn't already have high confidence then you wouldn't be in the sort of role (or applying for the sort of role) that requires that you speak in public. All my clients, without exception, are successful, confident people. They are high-achieving, go-to people, popular and out-going. At least, that's the outward impression.

How they feel about themselves, their 'self-esteem', may be quite different, however. Typically, they express a worry that they may not be able to live up to other people's expectations. They worry that they may not know as much about their profession as they think they should. They are terrified of making a mistake in front of people they respect and this fear stops them from taking risks as often as they would like to.

Self-esteem and negative self-talk

Self-esteem and confidence are different in one crucial way. Confidence is a measure of how you feel about your *abilities*. Self-esteem is how you feel about *yourself*. For instance, you might be aware that you're a good tennis player, but thoughts about how good other tennis players are may lead you to decide that you're 'not good enough' to perform at competition level.

Low self-esteem is the voice inside your head (also known as your 'self-talk') that says, "You will never be as good as that other person, so don't bother trying" or "No one is interested in what you have to say". The tragedy of low self-esteem is that we too easily believe our own negative self-talk even when those around us assure us of our abilities and potential.

We all compare ourselves to other people. On the one hand, we might choose to feel inspired by a person we admire and use their success in a positive way by setting ourselves a goal to be as good as they are. On the other hand, we may choose to feel intimidated by the success of someone else and tell ourselves that we will never be as good as they are so we might as well not try. Notice I used the word 'choose' in both of those examples. I believe that we have a choice. We can choose to be inspired and to do our best or we can choose to be despondent and not bother trying. Which choice you decide to make will have a tremendous impact on your success as a public speaker.

What follows is one of many exercises in this book that encourage you to be aware of your negative self-talk and to raise your self-esteem.

GIVE IT A GO! 7
Noticing negativity

Write a list of the personal qualities that other people have told you that you have.

Keep writing for as long as you can. I am sure you will write a long list.

When your list is complete, draw a circle around any of the qualities you do not truly believe you possess.

Look at the qualities that you have circled and think about why you have circled these qualities in particular. These circled qualities are an indication of where the 'you' that other people see doesn't match with how you feel inside.

The qualities you doubt are an indication of the areas in your life where you have low self-esteem. They are probably also the subjects of your own negative self-talk.

What would it take for you to believe that you possess all of the qualities on your list?

Remember to watch the video at www.publicspeakingmojo.co.uk

How to have higher self-esteem

How does it feel to know that high self-esteem (thinking well of yourself) is just a simple choice away? High self-esteem is a set of positive beliefs about yourself that you can choose to have right now.

Your negative thoughts about yourself are often the result of negative experiences that your unconscious mind has held onto for so long that you have convinced yourself that they are not thoughts but facts. The negative experiences may have happened as long ago as childhood. They may have been trivial and you may not even be able to remember what caused them. However, your unconscious mind stores everything, good and bad, as if it is true. Usually, this is a good thing but sometimes it is unhelpful. For instance, if someone once told you that you are not a good speaker your unconscious mind may have stored this information as a true belief. As the years passed and the belief has gone unchallenged it has become stronger and stronger in your mind. Eventually you accepted what was once someone else's opinion as a fact.

Low self-esteem is not fixed, nor is it your destiny to always be someone with low self-esteem. It is very easy to allow yourself to think badly of yourself, to 'beat yourself up' and to be negative about what you are capable of doing. However, you can just as easily 'big yourself up' and choose to believe that what you know, what you are and what you have to offer is admired, respected and wanted by other people.

You have a choice

When someone tells you what they think of you, you have a choice about whether or not to believe them. You can thank them for their opinion but you don't have to agree with it. If you have already chosen to believe that you are a bland, uninteresting, uninspiring speaker, what happens if you decide to believe the opposite?

This is a question that I enjoy testing out on myself when I have self-doubt.

GIVE IT A GO! 8
A thankful mindset

Think about a situation you have experienced that was embarrassing or disappointing, one where you didn't perform as well as you had hoped to.

Perhaps you did not win a pitch for new business that you had expected to or in an exam got a lower mark than you had wanted. Maybe a conversation with someone left you feeling bad about yourself.

Now imagine the scenario again but with a different mindset, one that acknowledges and is thankful for all that you learned through that experience; one that believes that there really is no 'failure' in life, only opportunities to learn and improve.

How different would life be (and how different would you feel) if you chose to believe in your own worth?

Imagine if you approached public speaking with the belief that you are taking steps on a journey to becoming a truly great speaker.

Remember to watch the video at www.publicspeakingmojo.co.uk

You win some, you lose some

Sometimes you will find public speaking truly rewarding. Other times it will just be frustrating. Yet every time you speak in public there will be valuable lessons that will help you to take another step up the ladder to becoming a really great speaker. What happens if you choose to feel good about your performance regardless of whether or not your presentation went exactly to plan?

If friends and family cannot help you become a better public speaker who can help you? You. You can help you.

Chapter Six

Change means growth (and growth hurts!)

> "When you become comfortable with uncertainty, infinite possibilities open up in your life."
>
> — ECKHART TOLLE —

Where will you find success?

There's a cliché in coaching circles that endures: success is just one step outside your comfort zone. Put this way change sounds quite easy, but change means growth and growth always hurts a bit. Fear of this 'growing pain' keeps many people in their comfort zone, even when they are very unhappy there. Most people know what is required to get to a better place but are too afraid to make the change. So they stay where they are, often unhappy and unfulfilled.

Stop wishing and start working

To get your public speaking mojo back you must stop wishing and start working. Just like building muscle the process will hurt a bit. For some, the discomfort is only mild. Once you have made the decision to change and commit to doing what it takes to ensure the change actually happens, everything that follows seems to flow quite easily, effortlessly and painlessly.

For others, every step on the journey is awkward and painful. However, the reward that you will receive at the end of your journey is more than worth it and the pain is soon forgotten. Keep in mind the many benefits of being a great public speaker (including raised profile, leadership opportunities and the chance to educate and inform) and any discomfort will be far easier to endure.

Responsibility, decision, commitment, action

To get your public speaking mojo back forever you will move through four key stages.

1. Responsibility

You lost your mojo. Only you can get it back.

Resist the temptation to blame others when things go wrong and accept that it is your responsibility to work towards becoming a great public speaker. You will need to call on other people for help and support from time-to-time. However, each step along the way is down to you alone.

2. Decision

This is the most difficult step. You may resist making decisions in other areas of your life because you fear the work that is ahead. However, indecision is not a good mental or emotional state to live in for very long. It can result in stress and sometimes even illness.

Whether you decide that you are going to work to get your public speaking mojo back or decide that you would rather everything in your life stayed just the way it is, make a decision and move yourself on from the discomfort of indecision. The moment you make a decision will be the moment you begin to feel better. So don't procrastinate a moment longer because there really is no need for delay. Whatever you decide will be the right decision for you (and you can always change direction again if you wish to), but do make a decision.

3. Commitment

Once you have made your decision the next step is to commit to it. You will find it most helpful to write your commitment down and then tell other people about it.

When my clients begin working with me the first thing I ask them to do is to tell other people that they are a public speaker. By making this declaration in public you are taking the first step on the road to truly believing it yourself.

Commitment matters. Without commitment you will never be any further forward than you are now.

4. Action

Although action can be a scary prospect, when you begin to take practical steps towards your goal you will be rewarded immediately with the feelings of pleasure that come with achievement. It may take several months to get your public speaking mojo back completely, and that is absolutely fine. Set yourself a realistic timescale and achievable goals. The more action you take and the more goals you achieve the more confident and happy you will feel.

Accept responsibility, make a decision, commit yourself to it and take action.

It really is this simple.

Just say 'Yes'

It is very tempting to say 'No' or 'Not now' to change when your life is very busy or if the steps you need to take are not immediately obvious to you. Right now, you may be finding it very difficult to imagine yourself as a confident public speaker. It feels easier, safer and more sensible to do nothing about it and to stay exactly where you are. If this is the approach that you have always taken when faced with challenging decisions I wonder what joys, failures and learning opportunities you may have missed.

As genuinely frightening as it may be, a challenge accepted is a wonderful opportunity for growth. In my own life, I live by one simple rule: say 'Yes' and think about how I am going to do it later.

You live in a fast-paced world. You probably work in a highly competitive industry. If you are slow to say 'Yes' to the opportunities that are presented to you then it is highly likely that someone else will get there first, leaving you with relief but also regret.

Next time you are offered the opportunity to speak in public, just say 'Yes'. Don't concern yourself with what you will talk about or how your presentation will flow. Just say 'Yes' and commit yourself, even though you don't feel ready. Choose to believe you have the ability to prepare no matter how much preparation time you are given. Dealing with the detail of what you will speak about and how you will present your ideas comes afterwards. You are not required to be ready right now. Say 'Yes' to the opportunity and concern yourself with the details in the days and weeks ahead.

GIVE IT A GO! 9
Say 'Yes'

Make a list of the questions that keep you from saying 'Yes' to an opportunity to speak in public. To start you off, here are a few of my own:
Am I good enough?
Do I know enough?
Do I have enough time to prepare?
Will people think I am an idiot for accepting this opportunity?
Will people be interested in what I have to say?
Will the other speakers be better than me?

Consider each question in turn and ask yourself: 'What would happen if I said 'Yes' to the opportunity anyway?'

Remember to watch the video at www.publicspeakingmojo.co.uk

You will always find it easy to invent reasons or excuses to say 'No' to a speaking opportunity. Be brave. Say 'Yes', and believe that from 'Yes' everything else will fall into place.

No one is perfect

There are no perfect public speakers. We all occasionally stumble over our words, forget bits or let our enthusiasm get the better of us and speak for longer than our allotted time. Public speaking is not about perfection. It is about interaction and the creation of a forum for new perspectives, ideas and debate.

There are many videos of wonderful presentations by fantastic speakers on the TED website (www.ted.com), on YouTube (www.youtube.com) and on Vimeo (www.vimeo.com). Yet people still turn out in all weathers to watch a public speaker because they enjoy the excitement of watching a presentation 'in person'. Give up the quest for perfection and commit to getting out in front of an audience again as soon as you possibly can.

Why it is vital to set goals

Goal-setting may sound boring. However, if you don't set goals then how will you know for certain that you have arrived where you want to be?

We often resist setting goals because deep inside we don't believe we are capable of achieving them. As a public speaking coach I can spot right away those new clients who haven't made a commitment to moving beyond their past experiences and who are not interested in setting goals. They don't want to solve their problem; they just want someone else to join them in their misery and inertia.

GIVE IT A GO! 10
What do you do?

One of the first goals I set my clients is this: Next time a stranger asks you what you do for a living say, "I am a public speaker".

Watch how they react.

Do they doubt you or simply believe you?

Remember to watch the video at www.publicspeakingmojo.co.uk

You may not feel ready to believe that you are a public speaker, yet the people you say it to may be ready to believe it very happily! You are not telling a lie. You are well on your way to becoming a great public speaker. However, you will get there more quickly if you start telling the world, and yourself, that you are a public speaker right now. Give the exercise a go and empower yourself in this very simple way.

Chapter Seven

We can be heroes: why it's your duty to perform

> ## "Hero isn't a noun, it's a verb."
>
> — ROBERT DOWNEY JNR —

A duty, but not a chore

As a disability rights campaigner, I value public speaking as a powerful tool for making a difference in the world. You can write heart-felt letters and emails and Tweets to influential people all day long but the response will probably disappoint you. When I discovered that I could reach so many more people in a much more direct and personal way by becoming a public speaker, I was hooked!

Thanks to public speaking I have had the privilege of seeing so many people become enthusiastic, loyal and active supporters of the causes I promote. Only when they see my enthusiasm, witness my knowledge and hear my arguments live and in person do people truly begin to understand what I'm campaigning for and what they can do to make a difference.

There is nothing more invigorating or rewarding than knowing that you have the ability to change a person's mind, educate them and convert them to a cause. Public speaking achieves all of this.

The value of your knowledge

Think about it. From the moment you were born other people invested in your knowledge and your education. From your earliest moments your family helped you to acquire language and the ability to use it to communicate how you feel, what you think and what you want. Your family encouraged your curiosity about the world. You asked a lot of questions and they shared their knowledge with you. Through school, university, work, the media and all the friendships, relationships and interactions you have had with other people throughout your life the depth, and the value, of your knowledge has grown.

As an adult, you may be fortunate enough to have the kind of job that allows you to make really good use of your skills and knowledge. If you don't have a job that you find personally fulfilling then perhaps you have found an alternative way to enjoy making use of what you know, through a hobby for instance, or through voluntary work. What you have learned about your profession and personal interests over the course of your life amounts to a lot of valuable knowledge.

You may not know as much about your subject as a university professor but you know a great deal more than most people ever will. With so much invested in you would you agree that you have a duty to share what you know with people who might benefit?

GIVE IT A GO! 11
Your valuable knowledge

Think of all the hobbies and interests you have had
during your childhood and since you became an adult.

Think of how many hours you have invested in your
hobbies and interests.

If you could place a monetary value on the skills and
knowledge that you have acquired over the years, what
would it be?

Remember to watch the video at www.publicspeakingmojo.co.uk

'No one is interested in what I have to say'

One of our greatest fears is rejection. When we are afraid
that people will say we are bad at public speaking we
invent excuses to avoid doing it. The most popular excuse
I hear is this: 'No one is interested in what I have to say'.

Isn't it sad when you meet someone who has talent but
no belief in themselves? Perhaps you have a friend or
relative who expresses regret that they weren't more
courageous when they had the opportunity to do what
they truly wanted to with their life. If you are reluctant to
share what you know through the medium of public
speaking then now is the time to wake yourself up to the
fact that you are one of these people. It is a great shame

because the world is missing out on what only you have to give.

Time for some tough talk

'No one is interested in what I have to say' isn't a fact. It's a little lie that you tell yourself so that you can avoid the risk of rejection. The truth is that many people will be interested in what you have to say. However, your fear of being rejected feels stronger than your belief that you can help people. So you choose fear and take the side of the lie.

When you lie to yourself you create a conflict in your mind that can lead to stress and even illness. You may think that you are safer in your 'comfort zone' but this state of fear and denial is not comfortable. The longer you stay in this state the more uncomfortable you will feel. However, when you decide to discover the truth about a situation and act on the truth instead of the lie your feelings of discomfort will begin to subside.

The truth is that many people will be very interested in what you have to say. 'No one is interested…' is not a valid excuse. It is a lie that you tell yourself because you are afraid to change. This simple revelation can be life-changing. My friend the author Martin Gladdish has written a wonderful book about this common malaise. It is called 'The Lazy Optimist'. I highly recommend it if you know that you make excuses to avoid moving out of your comfort zone.

The lies you tell yourself because you're scared

'No one is interested in what I have to say' may be just one of many lies that you have convinced yourself is true because you are afraid to move out of your comfort zone. Here is a list of other very common lies that people tell themselves because the lies enable them to avoid making a change. I am sure some of them are familiar to you. Perhaps you can add a few lies of your own to the list (if you do, challenge yourself to replace them with the truth).

The Lie I Tell Myself	The Truth
No one is interested in what I have to say.	Some people are very interested in what I have to say.
People cleverer than me will think I am an idiot so I am going to keep quiet!	People cleverer than me will benefit enormously from my unique perspective if I speak up.
I always perform badly because I am not good at speaking in front of others.	My performance is really good when I commit to preparing myself in the right way.
Whatever I do my nerves will always get the better of me.	I know how to use my 'nervous energy' to make my performance really great.
I hate the sound of my own voice. I am sure no one enjoys listening to it.	My voice is my tool and I will learn how to use it to greatest effect. Fortunately for me, my unique sound is memorable.
Everyone is judging me on how I look.	People are more interested in what they can learn from me than the way I look.

Believe that you deserve to be heard

GIVE IT A GO! 12
Whose voice do you hear?

Many fascinating people choose not to believe that they are interesting or 'good enough' and will not speak in public because they do not believe they 'deserve' to be heard.

If this sounds like you ask yourself these questions:
1. How did that disbelieving, self-deprecating voice in your head get there?
2. Is it your voice or someone else's?
3. Why do you allow it to be so powerful?
4. Is it stopping you from doing something you enjoy or being the person you really want to be?
5. What would happen if you decided not to believe the voice?

Remember to watch the video at www.publicspeakingmojo.co.uk

Having made the 'duty' of public speaking sound very serious, let's make it fun.

When the duty becomes a joy

I understand that for many people speaking in public is a necessary evil, a miserable and thankless task that you've been coerced into by a manager or family member. 'It will be 'character-building'', they insist.

Given that speaking can be a source of stress it seems perfectly sensible that you might wish to avoid it, particularly if you are still recovering from a bad past experience. What I am about to tell you may put some of the joy back into public speaking as it will reconnect you to the pleasure of 'performing'.

What I learned about performance from 1980s pop

I am a child of the 1980s, a decade now regarded as a golden age for pop music. My pop idols were flamboyant, colourful and charismatic.

I was aged ten when pop/punk pioneers Adam & the Ants exploded onto the music scene. Adam Ant was a huge influence on me and can take credit for helping me to believe that I had something to say that the world might find interesting or inspiring. He is an iconic entertainer who puts performance above everything else. More than thirty years later, Adam Ant's performances are still electrifying.

GIVE IT A GO! 13
Antmusic!

Putting personal musical tastes aside, log onto YouTube and search for any 1980s performance by Adam & the Ants.

Notice the commitment and the energy that Adam Ant and his band put into every performance.

What lessons can you take from Adam?

Are there any elements of his stage performance that you might bring to your public speaking performance?

Remember to watch the video at www.publicspeakingmojo.co.uk

Public speakers are not like pop stars though... are they?

While you may not have a talent for singing there are three key ways that public speakers are just like pop stars.

1. You engage

You must have heard the phrase 'to hold the audience's attention'. However, it takes some skill to keep the people in your audience interested and comfortable for longer than a few minutes. We humans are very easily distracted. During your presentation the attention of the people in your audience may become diverted for any number of reasons, for instance, by someone entering the room or by a disturbance, such as noise in the street outside. The most dangerous and ever-present distraction of all, however, is your audience members' own internal dialogue.

When you say something of interest, the people in your audience will shift the focus of their attention inwardly from what you are saying to their own thoughts about what you just said. When deep in thought they are no longer listening to you. Similarly, if they write a note or post something about your presentation on social media their attention will become focussed on what they are doing and no longer focussed on you.

While you are speaking be sure to cast your eyes around the room from time-to-time to check that you are maintaining the attention of the people in your audience. If you don't make this effort then they may lose the thread of what you are saying and may even miss some of your key points. It is part of your job as the speaker to constantly re-engage the people in your audience with the content of your presentation.

What can you do to bring the focus of their attention back to you? Should you stop speaking, make a sudden loud noise or stare at anyone who doesn't appear to be paying enough attention? These tactics may work in a classroom of distracted children but are not appropriate for adults.

Fortunately, there are a number of very simple techniques that you can deploy to keep the people in your audience engaged without making them feel they have misbehaved.

↷ **Tell a story.** People love stories. By creating a 'narrative arc' (a story) within your talk you can get everyone 'hooked'. The more drama and twists you put in your story the easier you will find it to keep everyone's attention.

⚐ **Use the energy.** Notice the energy level in the room and use your voice and movement to increase or decrease the energy. People appreciate variety. By varying your energy you will help the people in your audience to remain interested in you.

⚐ **Show your enthusiasm.** If you aren't enthusiastic about your subject you can hardly expect the people in your audience to be. When you smile, look pleased to be there, and tell them how much you appreciate this opportunity to speak to them they will reward you with their attention.

2. You perform

All presentations should be a performance. However, there is good performance and there is bad performance. Good performance happens 'in this moment'. When you are performing well you are completely aware of the people in your audience, the flow of communication and the exchange of energy, as it passes back and forth between you. The name for this set of conditions is 'presence' (more about presence in Chapter 11).

Bad performance happens when you disengage from 'what is happening now' (the present) and immerse yourself in fantasy, as if the people in your audience are passive observers rather than active participants. You may have seen this happen when you have watched other speakers at work. The speaker breaks eye contact with the people in the audience and starts speaking to him or herself almost as if he or she is an actor performing one of Shakespeare's soliloquies.

Public speakers differ from actors in one key aspect: actors never deviate from the script. They perform in front of an audience but rarely react to it. Public speakers use their 'script' merely as a guide, your main focus being the reaction of the people in the audience to the content you are delivering.

3. You inspire

What inspires people? A great idea or a moving story might be described as 'inspiring'. However, to be truly inspirational you must move the people in your audience to act. This is a challenge. Sympathy or understanding without action isn't of much use to you.

As a speaker you have a purpose: to inspire the people in your audience to 'act' in some meaningful way.

To be truly inspiring you must give the people in your audience at least one unambiguous 'call to action'. Tell them in as much detail as is necessary exactly what it is you want them to do. If you are clear and concise and able to show them how their action will lead directly to positive results then it is very likely that they will do what you ask.

If you are not sure whether you have the ability to inspire remember these really simple tactics that all inspirational speakers use:

Clarity and simplicity. Use plain language and ensure your 'call to action' is simple and unambiguous. Remember this very useful phrase: a confused mind says no!

Understanding. Check that the people in your audience have understood you. Be vigilant for signs of confusion (for example, they may start talking amongst themselves to get clarification from one another on what you just said). Nod at them. If they don't automatically nod back it may be a sign that they aren't following you.

Repeat yourself. Re-state your 'calls to action' at least three times throughout your presentation so that everyone has ample chance to hear them.

Hand-outs. Consider handing out materials at the end of your presentation that provide more information about your 'calls to action'. Keep these simple. Don't hand them out before or during your presentation (the people in your audience have enough distractions).

Questions. Invite questions about your 'calls to action'. This can be a great way of finding out whether what you have said has been understood.

It is your ego, the part of you that wants to be the cleverest person in the room, which seeks to complicate your messages. When you are comfortable on stage it is surprisingly tempting to want to show the people in your audience how clever you are. However, doing so won't help them to understand your message and won't enable them to follow your 'calls to action'.

Asking the people in your audience to do something for you is not enough. Be sure to ask them to do something they are capable of doing quickly and easily. You may be surprised by how eagerly they respond to a simple request that is clearly expressed.

Channel your inner pop star

This is a powerful technique that will help you to become a channel for your message.

When you give a presentation don't be yourself! At least, don't be the person you are in everyday conversation. The 'normal' version of you is too understated (too quiet, too modest) for the stage. To be a channel for a powerful message requires a powerful, charismatic performance.

This is your opportunity to put into practice what you learned from Adam Ant (or your own favourite pop star).

GIVE IT A GO! 14
A lesson in 'channelling'

Choose someone whose performances inspire you. It could be a pop star, actor or sportsperson.

Think about what it is about them you admire and makes you feel inspired.

Is it the way they stand? Their gestures? The way they talk?

The next time you rehearse a presentation give yourself permission to 'channel' some of the personal qualities, mannerisms and gestures of your hero.

Do not attempt an impersonation! This is still very much 'you'. Imagine what it feels like to be that person and borrow some of their inspirational energy (they won't know and they won't mind!).

Notice how you feel when you channel the energy of someone you admire.

Do you feel more confident?

More energetic?

More sure of yourself?

Remember to watch the video at www.publicspeakingmojo.co.uk

Had I not been exposed to the flamboyance and confidence of performers like Adam Ant when I was young I'm not sure I would have grown up to be the confident speaker that I am today.

No teacher ever encouraged me to be a public speaker. It wasn't until I started my degree that presentation skills became something new that I realised I should master. The confidence and expertise that I have now enable me to help other people with their confidence and so the inspiration I took from Adam Ant continues to inspire me, thirty years after I first discovered him.

Chapter Eight

Are you sitting too comfortably? Re-discover your courage and drive

> ## "The safe decision has danger written all over it."
>
> — PAUL ARDEN —

What if...

What if the person who most inspires you never existed? What if everyone you came into contact with during your formative years discouraged you from developing your communication skills? What if you grew up believing that you should keep quiet and not share your knowledge with the world?

It is a sad fact that some of us receive less encouragement during childhood than others. Fortunately, it is really easy to give that encouragement to yourself right now.

GIVE IT A GO! 15
'I am a great public speaker'

Say the following phrases to yourself, either in your head or out loud (if you are alone!):

'I am a great public speaker'

'People are very interested in what I have to say'

'I can help others by sharing what I know'.

You may find it difficult to believe these words the first few times you say them, however much you would like to.

Establish a daily routine so that you say these phrases to yourself at least twice a day, perhaps just after you brush your teeth.

Your unconscious mind, that part of your brain that holds your deep-seated beliefs about yourself, is like a sponge, quick to absorb whatever you tell it. When you repeatedly tell your unconscious mind lots of positive things about yourself it will eventually accept them as truths.

Give it a go for a few weeks. You may be amazed when you begin to notice how you feel about yourself is changing for the better.

Remember to watch the video at www.publicspeakingmojo.co.uk

Moving out of your comfort zone

Modern life is often hectic and can be stressful. It is tempting to settle for a job that demands less from you than to risk making your life more complex and demanding by trying something new.

However, stay where you feel comfortable for too long and you will eventually begin to feel restricted. To feel happy and content we need to grow, intellectually, emotionally and psychologically. There is no space for growth inside your 'comfort zone'. Its walls are solid and will only allow for things to stay as they are.

You may feel, as so many people do, that you're 'not good enough' to move up in life. You may feel that people cleverer or more 'deserving' than you will mock you if you try to improve yourself and you know that you will find their negativity hurtful and difficult to deal with. You may feel worried that other people (such as your partner or friends) will no longer like you if you change.

However, remaining within the confinement of your comfort zone is also risky. People who are untested or unfulfilled often feel disappointed by life. They tend to be unhappy in their work and find any change difficult. The ability to face change positively, even when it scares you, may mean you soon find yourself in a much happier state of mind, more confident in your own abilities and more able to help other people.

Every successful person has, at some time in their life, found it difficult to move out of their comfort zone. Many have stayed there far too long and with hindsight regret their lack of courage. If you have never done anything that scares you and know you have never tried to move out of your comfort zone, where can you find the motivation to get moving?

Finding your drive

When I was younger, I didn't have very high self-esteem and I would never willingly put myself forward as a public speaker (I had the talent but not the belief). I only discovered how much I could love public speaking when a manager forced me to do it! I was very angry with him at the time, but am so grateful to him now because he helped me to discover my passion. My only regret is that I didn't discover it sooner.

These days, I find it quite easy to challenge myself. When faced with a difficult decision about whether or not I should move out of my comfort zone I ask myself this: what will happen if I do nothing?

If the answer to that question is 'some people will be worse off' then I know I have to act. This may sound altruistic but it has more to do with my personal drive than a desire to do good. I am highly motivated by helping other people. When I help other people it makes me feel good. All effort seems worthwhile if someone else benefits.

This is what drives me. What drives you?

GIVE IT A GO! 16
Risk assessment

Take a few minutes to think about a time when you found complete satisfaction from a task that required you to take a personal risk in order to fully complete it.

Altruism (doing something selflessly) doesn't necessarily involve risk. Risk is when you stand to lose something that is of value to you (this could be your time, your reputation or something more tangible such as money or possessions).

Remember the decision-making process that you went through when you decided that taking that risk was the right thing to do.

How did you feel afterwards? Did the risk pay off and if so how?

Now imagine that you had decided not to take the risk for fear of negative consequences.

What consequences did your inaction have for you and for other people?

Who failed to benefit from your unique gifts because you decided to hold back?

Remember to watch the video at www.publicspeakingmojo.co.uk

It is perfectly okay to say 'No' to moving out of your comfort zone sometimes, particularly if you have other pressing responsibilities (such as children). However, it is also important to be aware of the consequences of saying 'No' and to be really honest with yourself about why you are saying 'No' (for example, are you using your children as an excuse?). The 'No' that is driven by fear may be the 'No' that stands in the way of your own personal growth and the prosperity of other people.

Who will find the cure for cancer?

One of the reasons people avoid the opportunity to speak in public is because they believe the people in the audience are superior to them. They believe that if they have the audacity to step onto a stage in front of these people they will be immediately exposed as fraudulent. If this sounds familiar then I would like to help you look at the situation in a different way.

Rather than focus on what you feel are your own inadequacies, pause to reflect with compassion on the inadequacies that the clever, experienced, successful people in your audience may have.

- Their subject knowledge may not be as up-to-date as yours

- They may have forgotten a few things and welcome the reminder

- They may experience self-doubt and appreciate hearing from another professional who can confirm what they believe is correct

- They may welcome the challenge to their own ideas

- They may rarely have the opportunity to hear about their subject from anyone other than their immediate peers

- They may experience a 'penny-drop' moment following months or years of trying and failing to find a solution

When considered from this perspective the case for speaking in front of people who may be more knowledgeable than you becomes a lot more attractive. You may believe that you are being judged when, in truth, it is you who is unfairly judging the people in your audience.

Creating those 'eureka' moments

Public speakers do far more than share knowledge. We create an environment where people can reflect on what *they* know.

Through their reflections the people in the audience can arrive at conclusions or realisations about their own work that they have been struggling to reach for years. I call these 'eureka' or 'lightbulb' moments. Wouldn't it be a tragedy if the solution to one of humanity's greatest problems remained undiscovered because you decided not to believe that anyone would be interested in what *you* have to say?!

GIVE IT A GO! 17
Facing up

This will take courage!

Find an opportunity to speak in front of an audience of people whom you know are more intelligent, experienced or successful than you (I find university lecturers or scientists work best!).

Notice how they react to you.

Do they ask questions?

Do they approach you afterwards and if so what do they say?

How do you feel afterwards?

Remember to watch the video at www.publicspeakingmojo.co.uk

Take a few leaves from the book of your hero

There are many reasons why I admire and draw energy and encouragement from my heroes. Highly creative performers don't ask the world's permission before they perform. They have a creative idea, develop it and share it. If their idea isn't received in the way they were hoping then they try a new approach.

Remember that you can draw a great deal of encouragement from your hero's attitude towards risk, creativity and performance. It is time to re-frame your relationship with fear and to approach public speaking with greater compassion for the unexpressed needs of the people in your audience. When you do, the positive impact on the world can be huge.

Chapter Nine

Mojo: a state of mind and body working in harmony

> "The rhythm of the body,
> the melody of the mind and
> the harmony of the soul
> create the symphony of life."
>
> — B.K.S. IYENGAR —

The power of your thoughts

Your mind is extremely powerful. You can conjure thoughts and ideas from nowhere, find solutions to complex problems and invent new and ingenious ways to make your world better. This is wonderful news, especially if you know how to harness this power to your advantage.

Unfortunately, negative thoughts can be even more powerful than positive ones. Negative thoughts about yourself as a speaker are the reason you lost your public speaking mojo. By allowing thoughts about a few negative experiences to overpower your mind, you succeeded in convincing yourself that you are not, and cannot be, a great public speaker. If you continue to think about your ability in this negative way you won't allow yourself to try public speaking again and you will never get your mojo back!

How you think about yourself and the extent to which you are able to challenge and change your negative thoughts is the difference between getting your public speaking mojo back for good and losing it forever.

The 'F' word

I don't like to talk about the 'F' word: fear.

When I start to talk about fear you soon start to think about fear. When you start to think about fear you soon start feeling fear. While there is no need for fear in this situation (public speaking isn't usually dangerous) it may be helpful to reflect on why the thought of speaking in public can make you feel fearful. It is all to do with your ancient past.

Fear of public speaking: is it natural?

You were born with just two natural fears. Fear of public speaking wasn't one of them. If fear of falling and fear of loud noises are the only fears you were born with why does fear of public speaking rank so highly on so many people's lists of phobias?

Some anthropologists believe that fear of public speaking may be a throwback to the way we lived several thousands of years ago. Back in our hunter/gatherer days food was scarce. It was vital to your survival that you stayed within your social group. To separate yourself from your group was to put yourself at risk of being attacked by either an animal or by someone from another group, and if you couldn't find food on your own you could starve!

As a public speaker you stand alone facing a group of strangers. Is it possible that your brain recalls your ancient past and wrongly identifies the public speaking platform as a place of danger?

GIVE IT A GO! 18
Your ancient past

Think about what it would have been like for your ancestors whose survival depended on remaining part of a group.

Now think about how you live today.

You now live in an 'information age'. What we know is valuable and what we are willing and able to share with others can enable all of us to thrive.

Notice how this realisation makes you feel.

Is it a liberating thought?

Are you beginning to see why fear of public speaking is an unnatural fear that serves no purpose in the modern age?

Remember to watch the video at www.publicspeakingmojo.co.uk

Three more 'F' words

Adrenalin is the hormone that your brain tells your body to produce to prepare you for action. You may have been encouraged to think of adrenalin as the 'fight or flight' hormone. However, there is a third 'F' associated with adrenalin and it is one that public speakers are all too familiar with: 'freeze'.

Adrenalin is produced when your brain believes you are

in danger. This primal response was appropriate thousands of years ago when your chances of being attacked by a predator were a lot more realistic than they are today.

You are familiar with the rushing sensation of an adrenalin 'surge' in your body. Usually, you will feel an adrenalin surge when your brain identifies that you could be in mortal danger. The release of adrenalin is your brain's warning to you that you need to stand and fight, run away, or stay very still until the danger has passed. This makes perfect sense if you are confronted by someone waving a gun at you, but why does your brain tell your body to pump out so much adrenalin when you're about to speak in public?

Think back to what you have learned about the way your ancient ancestors survived. Your brain may still believe that standing in front of a large group of people who are not from your own social group is dangerous. So it tells your body to release adrenalin in an effort to make you run away, which is clearly an inappropriate response in this circumstance!

A little bit of adrenalin, that feeling of 'butterflies in the stomach', gives you a burst of energy that can enhance your performance. However, too much can ruin your performance as the sensation of too much adrenalin in your body is unpleasant. Is there a way to make use of your adrenalin so that it works for you rather than against you?

Adrenalin is a warning message from your brain to your body. If you try to ignore the warning your brain will instruct your body to produce even more adrenalin to make the warning louder! To let your brain know that you got the message and that it doesn't need to produce any more adrenalin right now, all you need to do is 'acknowledge and act'.

Have you noticed that when you start giving your presentation you begin to feel less anxious? This is because your 'action' (when you started to speak) has been noticed by your brain which interprets it as a sign that you have responded to its warning so it can now 'turn off the alarm'.

So the best thing to do if you feel your adrenalin pumping before your talk is to recognise what's going on in your body and start your talk! Try it, and notice how everything seems to calm down once you are on stage speaking.

GIVE IT A GO! 19
Adrenalin

Acknowledge: The next time you are about to give a presentation or attend an important meeting where you will be expected to speak spend a few minutes noticing the physical changes in your body.

You may notice a rush of energy.
Your heart may start to beat a little faster than normal.
Whatever you notice is normal for you.

Some people experience increased perspiration.

Others may notice their breathing has become faster and shallower.

These are all signs that your adrenalin is surging.

You may experience one of these signs, all of them or even more.

Act: Your rush of adrenalin is a sign that your body is getting ready to make a great performance. Your brain has given the cue, now it's your turn to act.

Your response to your rush of adrenalin is to start your pre-talk routine (see Chapter 12). Your pre-talk routine comprises any number of actions that you will take in the moments before you step on stage. The purpose of the routine is to let your body know that you acknowledge its 'call-to-action' and are about to act (so it can stop producing adrenalin now).

Remember to watch the video at www.publicspeakingmojo.co.uk

The 'C' word

As you prepare to make a presentation you might notice another sensation. It is like an adrenalin surge but a little less pleasant. It may cause an unwelcome feeling that some people describe as mild anxiety.

This less pleasant sensation is caused by the hormone cortisol (sometimes known as the 'stress hormone'). Cortisol helps your body to deal with stress by giving you a quick burst of energy just when you need it (so you can run away if necessary!). However, too much cortisol over a long period can cause things you definitely don't want, such as high blood pressure.

While just the right amount of adrenalin can help you to give a great performance cortisol is a little less helpful to you in this situation. You are preparing to speak, not to run away.

GIVE IT A GO! 20
Cortisol

Treat a pre-talk surge of cortisol in much the same way that you treat pre-talk adrenalin (see exercise #19), by treating it as a signal to begin your pre-talk routine.

Gently acknowledge the presence of cortisol in your body. In other circumstances, it would help you, but it is not needed for public speaking. Mentally thank cortisol for turning up for your presentation then compassionately let thoughts of it go from your mind.

Remember to watch the video at www.publicspeakingmojo.co.uk

Testosterone: why 'power poses' work

You now know that adrenalin and cortisol are helpful hormones but that they can cause you to feel uncomfortable if present in excessive amounts.

Fortunately, you have another helpful hormone that can enhance your public speaking performance and reduce the effects of cortisol in your body. It is easy to produce when you need it and it feels great! This hormone is testosterone (both men and women have it!).

So how do you increase your levels of testosterone and reduce your levels of cortisol quickly and safely at just the right time?

We now know exactly how to do this thanks to the pioneering work of social psychologist Amy Cuddy who is based at Harvard Business School in the United States. Through her pioneering research, Amy discovered that when you stand in a 'power pose' for as little as two minutes your body sends a message to your brain to produce more testosterone. The result is a feeling of increased power and reduced inhibition which is perfect for your public speaking performance.

GIVE IT A GO! 21
Power pose

The next time you are about to attend a meeting or speak at an event where you would usually feel a bit anxious or inhibited find a quiet room and stand in a 'power pose' for two minutes.

A popular 'power pose' is the 'Wonder Woman' pose.

To pose like the superhero Wonder Woman stand with your feet hip-width apart, place your fists on your hips with your elbow pointing outwards, push your shoulders back and tilt your head up.

If you don't fancy standing like Wonder Woman, choose any stance that makes your body bigger, such as athlete Usain Bolt's famous pre-competition pose. Alternatively, simply reach your arms up to the sky as if commanding the sun to shine.

IMPORTANT: Hold the pose for at least two minutes.

Watch Amy Cuddy's TED Talk 'Your Body Language Shapes Who You Are' on the TED website www.TED.com.

Remember to watch the video at www.publicspeakingmojo.co.uk

A word about 'highs'…

It's understandable that you may be tempted by the promises made by the manufacturers of so-called 'legal highs' in the belief that they will help your performance and reduce your feelings of anxiety. A 'high' may be anything from caffeine-enhanced products (energy drinks) to over-the-counter and prescription tablets.

None of these products is good for your self-esteem in the longer term as they can create a belief in your mind that you are only able to perform if you have taken a legal high. Furthermore, each brings with it health problems (in some cases mental health problems, in others physical problems) that will only serve to shorten your career as a public speaker.

Effective public speakers are fully present. Stimulants destroy presence because they divert your attention inwardly, away from the needs of the people in your audience. Whether it comes in a can or a pill avoid unnatural highs. Give the 'power pose' technique a go instead.

Open your eyes

When you have an aversion to a task that you can't avoid (cleaning the kitchen floor in my case), you may attempt to dissociate yourself from it by doing it with your eyes closed and your breath held. You avoid looking at what you're doing too closely and attempt to get it over with as quickly as possible. Once it is done you do your best to forget about it until the next time you have to do it. Mentally, you do all you can to put distance between yourself and the cause of your disgust or discomfort.

I have noticed that some reluctant public speakers do much the same thing. They avoid looking at the people in the audience by facing the projector screen or looking at the ceiling, the back of the room or the floor. They screw up their eyes and their expressions are pained. They barely breathe and mentally they are 'somewhere else'. Emotionally, they are dissociated from reality. These are the perfect conditions for poor performance.

Good performance requires presence (more about presence in Chapter 11). A key aspect of presence is your ability to look at your audience when you're talking to them.

Hold your gaze

If you find it difficult to make or maintain eye contact when talking to someone you may find it even more difficult to look out into a sea of faces when you're making your presentation. Eye contact is very powerful. It can also be extremely intimate. In fact, some people struggle to maintain eye contact because they find the intimacy too uncomfortable. However, eye contact is a key aspect of engagement so finding a way to overcome any discomfort around eye contact is important.

You may find eye contact difficult for a number of reasons. Eye contact may remind you of a bad experience with someone who used gaze to scare or control you. Eye contact can be a precursor to aggression (think how many drunken brawls have begun because one person took offence at the way the other person was looking at him or her). However, your gaze can also be an incredibly powerful tool for communication. Sometimes you can say as much with your eyes as you can with words. You can use your gaze to let the people in your audience know that they are included and that they are 'present', noticed and involved.

Some types of eye contact feel really good. Perhaps you have been to an event where one of your heroes was performing. For a split second his or her eyes met yours. What an exhilarating feeling! In the dating game eye contact is crucial. A meeting of eyes can be a signal of interest or desire.

Alternatively, if someone won't meet your gaze it may be a sign that they're not interested in you, or perhaps they are shy or feel intimidated.

If you can master your use of gaze it will transform you into a speaker with great charisma and presence. If this sounds unlikely experiment with eye contact and see what happens.

GIVE IT A GO! 22
Eye contact

If you find looking people in the eye uncomfortable, be brave and practise it the next time you are in a conversation with someone.

Do not attempt to engage them in a staring contest!

Look at them for a second longer than you would normally and increase the length of the eye contact the next time you talk to them.

Eye contact becomes more comfortable the more often you do it.

Notice how your conversations with people change when you use more eye contact.

Remember to watch the video at www.publicspeakingmojo.co.uk

Self-talk (the commentator inside your head)

We all have an 'internal commentator'. It is the voice inside your head that provides a running commentary on life that only you can hear. Unfortunately, your internal commentator has a lot of opinions about you and not all of them are complimentary.

This 'negative self-talk' happens when you allow bad thoughts about yourself to speak louder and more powerfully than your positive thoughts. Sometimes the disapproving commentator is your own voice telling you that you are not good enough, that you do not deserve success, that everyone thinks you are foolish or that you have nothing of value to say. Perhaps the negative commentator is someone from your past; a teacher, parent, employer or friend who told you that you had failed. Usually, the negative commentator is a combination of other people's voices, past experiences and your own self-doubt.

Negative self-talk is the ultimate self-fulfilling prophecy. When you tell yourself repeatedly that you are no good at something eventually you will start to believe it is the truth. You may have heard this quote by Henry Ford: 'Whether you think you can or you think you can't, you're right'. When you start to believe your own negative self-talk you start to live by it. Eventually your negative beliefs will manifest themselves in the symptoms of low self-esteem.

GIVE IT A GO! 23
True believer

If what you believe about yourself becomes what is true about yourself what happens when you make a decision to believe something more positive?

Develop a habit of challenging your beliefs about yourself. Notice how challenging your negative beliefs changes how you feel about your ability to succeed.

Remember to watch the video at www.publicspeakingmojo.co.uk

Believe in yourself

You may have been told that if you would only believe in yourself you would realise what a great public speaker you are. However, it takes more than 'blind faith' to challenge and change a deeply-held belief.

To change the way you think about your ability as a public speaker you must first accept that what you believe about yourself is your free choice and that because it is your free choice you can choose, right now, to change what you believe.

GIVE IT A GO! 24
'I choose what I believe'

The following sentence may change your life forever so write it on a piece of paper and put it somewhere you will see it every day.

'I choose what I believe.'

Now add to this, **'I choose to believe that I am a talented public speaker.'**

Over the next few weeks, notice how the way you feel about these words changes.

Remember to watch the video at www.publicspeakingmojo.co.uk

This is powerful, life-changing stuff. If you think the exercise is too simple to make a difference do it and notice what happens. In any situation where your self-talk tells you that you are 'not good enough' gently remind yourself of this one, simple truth: you can choose what you believe.

GIVE IT A GO! 25
Challenge the negative

Grab a pen and paper and draw two columns.

In the column on the left make a list of all the negative things that you currently believe to be true about yourself.

The list can be as long as you like. It is private and will only be seen by you.

When you are ready, use the column on the right to reverse each negative statement.

For example, if you have written 'No one is interested in anything I have to say', you could reverse it to 'Someone will be interested in some of the things I have to say'.

Note my careful use of language. I did not write 'Everyone will be interested in everything I have to say' because this is not realistic. People have different interests and different levels of need, but in every audience there will be people for whom what you have to say will be both interesting and potentially life-changing. This is one of the great truths about public speaking and it is a truth that you can choose to believe right now.

Once you have completed column two, find a pair of scissors and cut the piece of paper in half vertically so that you have all your negative statements on one piece of paper and all your positive and realistic statements on another piece of paper. Now put the list of negative statements into a paper shredder because you have finished with it.

What you are now left with is a list of positive statements of what you can choose to believe about yourself from this moment forward.

Put this list somewhere you can easily see it and make an effort to read it aloud to yourself at least once a day for a month.

Remember to watch the video at www.publicspeakingmojo.co.uk

You may be surprised by how quickly you begin to believe these positive statements about yourself. When you start to believe them your behaviour will also begin to change in a positive way.

By keeping an eye on the note to yourself that reads 'I can choose what I believe' and your list of realistic statements your negative self-talk will become quieter and quieter. It may even disappear completely.

Breath support

Constantly and effortlessly your breath is your sure and steady companion through life. Over the centuries, people have used their own breath as the focus of their meditation practice. Wherever you go your breath goes with you. You don't have to search for it because it is always there.

For public speakers breath is of even greater significance because your breath supports the most important tool of your trade: your voice. To speak clearly and purposefully you need adequate breath. This is called 'breath support'.

GIVE IT A GO! 26
Breath support

Open a book or magazine at any page, take a deep breath down into your body and start reading aloud.

Keep going until that breath runs out and you can speak no more.

What do you notice about the quality of your speech as the seconds pass?

Does it maintain its power and resonance or does your voice become weaker?

Does it become difficult to pronounce words clearly?

Remember to watch the video at www.publicspeakingmojo.co.uk

As you have just discovered your speaking voice needs breath support to sound powerful and clear. When you get into a good habit of taking regular breaths during your presentations you will feel calmer and you will sound a great deal clearer too.

GIVE IT A GO! 27
Not on the 'in' breath

Return to that book or magazine and read aloud once more.

This time breathe normally but only speak on your 'in' breath.

Notice what happens to your voice this time.

Never speak while breathing in! Not only is it uncomfortable your words will be difficult for anyone to understand. So what should you do if you run out of breath mid-sentence? Simple: pause and take a breath.

There's no rule that says you have to squeeze every sentence inside the space of a single breath. If you attempt it you will probably run out of breath before the end of your sentence and become flustered and uncomfortable.

Remember to watch the video at www.publicspeakingmojo.co.uk

GIVE IT A GO! 28
Try a tongue-twister

The best way to get your breath support right is by practising your presentation. By doing so you will get a feel for how words, phrases and sentences form in your mouth and you will be able to tell how much breath you will need to support your speech.

Try it now with this tongue-twister.

Take a breath and read the line aloud, slowly and with as much passion as you can muster but do not take a second breath until you have finished the entire phrase.

'A big black bug bit a big black bear, made the big black bear bleed blood'

What was that like? Did you struggle?

Did you notice that you automatically took a couple of shallow breaths in an attempt to get to the end of the phrase?

Say the phrase again but this time pause and breathe after each line:

'A big black bug bit a big black bear,

made the big black bear bleed blood'

Did you find it easier this time? Did your speech sound clearer?

Remember to watch the video at www.publicspeakingmojo.co.uk

This kind of rehearsal really pays off. Notice how often you need to take a breath to support your words and make sure that you do. Start to think about your breath as a tool. Become preoccupied with how you will use your breath to support your words.

You can control your breathing for clear, understandable speech. You may have heard this described as 'phrasing'. Always practise 'speaking your presentation' before you perform it in front of an audience to ensure that you are aware of all the best places to take a breath.

The power of silence

It is a paradox, but the most effective public speakers are those who make the most effective use of silence. A 'comfortable silence' is nice, but an 'uncomfortable silence' is powerful!

Next time you rehearse a presentation experiment with silence. Hold a silence a couple of seconds longer than would usually be comfortable and notice the effect it has on the people in your audience. Anyone looking away will probably look up because an unexpected silence often signals danger!

Silence gives the people in your audience an opportunity to think, so build plenty of silences into your presentations.

Chapter Ten

The four elements beyond your control

> ## "You can't always control the wind, but you can control your sails"
>
> – TONY ROBBINS –

Those things outside your control

You and only you are responsible for the success of your presentation. However, a successful talk is dependent on a number of factors that you do not directly control, including the Chairperson, the other speakers, the audience and the environment. While you cannot control any of these factors there are a number of ways you can influence them.

The Chairperson

You would be forgiven for thinking Chairpeople have their speakers' best interests at heart. I'm sure they think they do. However, Chairpeople should come with a health-warning: likely to induce stress.

Count yourself very lucky if the person chairing your event is both experienced and fully prepared. Unfortunately, more often than not, the Chairperson has been called upon to moderate your session at the last minute, given very little information about the event, has never chaired a conference before and is more nervous than any of the speakers.

There are many ways a Chairperson can damage your presentation (if you let him!):

↬ He spends insufficient time talking to the speakers before the event starts, which means he doesn't know what you need (changes in lighting, for instance) to ensure your presentation runs smoothly.

↬ He gets your name wrong.

↬ He doesn't know who you are or what you have done and so introduces you inappropriately. At worst, he reads out the wrong biography or doesn't bother to introduce you at all ('Our next speaker needs no introduction…').

↬ He gives away the main points of your presentation.

↬ He lets the first speaker over-run, then gives all subsequent speakers a hard time if they refuse to under-run.

↬ He talks to other panel members while you're giving your presentation.

↬ He is over-zealous in his time-keeping, announcing how many minutes you have left throughout your talk at ten-minute intervals, thus interrupting your train of thought and breaking your audience's concentration.

↬ If there is a panel session he favours the person he knows/admires/is most intimidated by.

↬ The worst sin of all in my book: he gives the audience insufficient encouragement to ask questions.

Use your influence to ensure your Chairperson works for you and not against you.

↪ Find out who the Chairperson is before the day of the event and make an effort to get to know him. Social media is particularly useful for this.

↪ Make it your responsibility to let the Chairperson know exactly what you need to make your presentation as good as it can possibly be.

↪ Tell the Chairperson what your name is and how to pronounce it.

↪ Send your biography to the Chairperson personally in advance and take a printed copy with you on the day so he has no excuse for getting it wrong.

↪ Tell the Chairperson how you would like to be introduced. This is a very good idea if you have several different professional hats and a complex biography.

↪ Tell him explicitly what you don't want him to say in his introduction. For all you know the Chairperson may have heard you speak before and may inadvertently give your punchlines away, not out of spite but enthusiasm.

↪ On the issue of timing, if you are told that your timeslot has been reduced accept the fact graciously and continue to put on a great performance. You will be able to do this because you have deliberately planned to talk for ten per cent less than the allotted time in case of such an emergency.

↬ Here is a neat trick for keeping to time without constant interruptions from the Chairperson. Bring your own timer (the kind that beeps when time has run out) and set it in full view of the Chairperson and the people in your audience as you begin to speak. Everyone will then know that you are going to stick to time.

Tip: I use a 'kitchen timer'. I don't use my mobile phone's alarm because when I'm in full-flow I tend to ignore the sound of phones! The kitchen timer has a very distinct sound which my brain automatically associates with 'Stop talking now!' Don't rely on your watch or a clock. You may be surprised how difficult it is to read a watch or clock while you are speaking. It is far more effective to use a separate device that displays a countdown.

↬ If the Chairperson starts talking to other speakers while you are speaking you can probably rely on the people in your audience to give him the evil eye! You should 'play harder'. Show the people in your audience that you are the one taking their needs seriously. They will appreciate it very much.

↬ During a panel session, be forthright. Don't wait to be asked your opinion. Lean in, raise your hand slightly and interject. If you find this very difficult, touch the Chairperson on the arm (if he is within reach) or say to him, 'May I come in here?'

↬ If the Chairperson gives the people in the audience insufficient time to raise their hands with questions, intervene. I make a little speech to the audience to the effect that this is a rare chance for them to put me on the spot and they should grab it! If this doesn't work, I gently encourage them by adding that there are no 'stupid questions' and that other people in the audience will be very grateful to those who have the courage to ask something. This usually has the desired effect. Too few conferences give people in the audience the opportunity to 'confer'. This is something I'm keen to change!

The Other Speakers

The speakers who share a platform with you are temporarily your colleagues. Not that you would know it as you are rarely encouraged to think of them in this way. You might expect that when you arrive to speak at a conference one of the organisers will introduce you to the other speakers. In my experience this rarely happens. More often than not I find I need to take it upon myself to seek out and say 'hello' to the other speakers (they are invariably grateful when I do).

Public speaking can be quite lonely. You are surrounded by people and yet you are in many ways different to everyone else in the room with the exception of the other speakers. Make an effort with them. It is great to feel that you are part of an 'elite team'.

It is not a competition

Public speaking is not a competition (unless you are taking part in a public speaking competition!). Presentations should flow from one to the next giving the people in the audience an experience that feels like it has been put together with deliberate care. Rather than dwelling on how you can be 'better' that the person who speaks before you, your main focus should be on how you can complement the work of the other speakers to give the audience a 'blended' experience of light and shade.

Resist the urge to compare yourself unfavourably to the presenters you admire. You will feel frustrated with yourself if you come up short. Instead, draw inspiration from them and be the best that you can be. Take joy in knowing that you've now reached the level where you share a platform with someone who has inspired you. That is an amazing achievement. Develop your own authentic style and set your own achievable standard for excellence that has authenticity at its heart.

Fit yourself in

If the speaker before you is high energy match her energy level so the people in the audience don't experience a dip in energy and become restless or bored. If the speaker before you is low energy build your own energy gradually to the level at which you know you shine (don't bound onto the stage immediately after her like an excited puppy – that really is too much and wastes the opportunity you have to build your presentation's strength to a crescendo).

Spare a thought for the speaker who will follow you. One of the worst public speaking clichés is 'Well how do I follow that?!' Find out what kind of speaker the next speaker is and adjust your energy so that she doesn't feel completely out of place when she follows you. You may feel justified in showing the following speaker how great you are in comparison to her but the people in your audience may have a different perspective. Always be gracious.

Good grace

It is also gracious to compliment your fellow speakers on their knowledge and their style of presentation during your own talk. Make direct reference to points they have raised. The speakers concerned will glow with pride while the people in the audience will get the very positive impression that you are all working together as a team.

GIVE IT A GO! 29
Watch the speakers interact

Next time you are an audience member at a conference where there are a number of speakers notice how the speakers interact with one another.

Do they reference one another's talks?

When they do, how does this affect the atmosphere both on the stage and in the room?

Remember to watch the video at www.publicspeakingmojo.co.uk

The Audience

The people in your audiences rarely behave exactly as you expect them to. They are subdued when you expect a rabble, silent when you expect laughter and giggle when you weren't aware you had made a joke. They fidget and fiddle, look bored (even when they're enjoying every word of your presentation) and are particularly poor at letting you know when you're doing well. They don't ask questions except when you don't want them to. They don't listen. They talk to the person next to them in what they think is a whisper (it's not) and despite repeated requests they never switch their mobile phones to 'silent' (I suspect many people simply don't know how to).

I could continue this tirade but you might start to think I don't enjoy the company of the people in my audiences and that would be wrong because I love them. As frustrating and unpredictable as they can be the people who come to hear you speak are your opportunity. When they are gripped by an idea and know what they need to do to help you to realise your vision there is no stopping them. Getting them to that place is a joy. However, their cooperation isn't easily won and audience behaviour can be one of the reasons why people with only a little speaking experience lose their public speaking mojo.

Who are they really?

Your relationship with the people in your audience matters more than anything else. Your audience is a diverse group of individuals with emotions and prejudices that are affected by innumerable factors outside your control (and theirs!). What's more, the people in your audience don't know themselves very well. They are unable to express what they need from you because for the most part they simply don't know.

Your audience arrives at your event in full expectation that you will identify its needs and meet them to its full satisfaction. People bring with them anxieties that even they don't know they have. Your audience can cause an atmosphere to be uplifting or oppressive, welcoming and friendly or intimidating and overwhelming.

What do they want?

While you can ask the person who has organised the event who the people in the audience are and what it is they expect from you, you will never receive more than basic demographical information.

What you really need to know is:

↬ How much do they know already?

↬ What is their learning style?

↬ How are they feeling today?

Imagine how well your preparation and delivery would be informed if you had this information!

Unfortunately, it's impossible to know any of these things for sure. So it is up to you to take some educated guesses, research as much as possible and to be open to changing your presentation as it is happening if you detect that it is not meeting your audience's needs.

How to meet your audience's needs when no one has any idea what their needs are

The content of your talk is only part of the story. To meet the needs of the people in your audience as comprehensively as possible there are many more aspects of the public speaker's role to be mastered.

An awareness of how to conduct the energy in the room

You have witnessed great speakers and poor speakers. A key difference between them is energy. Great speakers seem to light up the room. They acknowledge that we live in an imperfect world but show determination to rise above our collective troubles to deliver a powerful and empowering message.

Poor speakers lack energy. They give the impression that they don't really care about the subject they're talking about which leaves the people in the audience feeling disappointed and uninspired.

So how can you generate energy?

⟡ By showing enthusiasm for your subject.

⟡ By showing genuine interest in the well-being of the people in your audience.

⟡ By asking searching questions and encouraging your audience to think.

GIVE IT A GO! 30
Positive energy

Next time you watch a speaker conduct positive energy in a room reflect on how he or she is achieving this.

Are there things this speaker is doing that you might bring to your own presentations?

Remember to watch the video at www.publicspeakingmojo.co.uk

End your presentation properly

Throughout this book I keep returning to the idea of 'responsibility'. It is your responsibility to ensure that all aspects of your presentation go well. This even extends to making sure you receive a round of applause at the end of your presentation.

Always make sure you get your applause. You may believe that only people on an ego trip need applause but this just isn't true. Applause sends a message to your brain that the 'performing' part of your presentation is now over enabling it to switch into a different, more conversational, mode. Your applause also tells your unconscious mind that all is well and that you did a good job. Hearing applause that is meant just for you will trigger a release of endorphins, those hormones that make you feel good.

When you have completed your presentation bow your head slightly and say 'Thank you'. This will cause the people in your audience to applaud automatically. If you don't give your audience this cue they may not applaud simultaneously and this will create a problem for you. You deserve your applause. It is your reward for a good job done well. If you don't get your reward you may start to doubt your performance. This doubt can very quickly become a negative belief about yourself as a speaker and negative beliefs are what caused you to lose your mojo in the first place.

Presence

Great speakers live in 'the now' (the present). They don't talk 'at' the people in their audience; they communicate 'with' them.

Overcome the invisible barriers

Have you ever noticed that sometimes the people in your audience appear to be disconnected from you? Do they behave as if they're watching you on television? This state of disconnection or 'dissociation' is brought about by the invisible barriers that are created by the conventional conference room format.

The typical conference arrangement stands the presenter in a (usually though not always) raised space at the front of the room with the audience in rows of chairs or around tables some distance away. These layout conventions create an invisible barrier between speaker and audience. It is important that you are aware of this barrier because you must ensure that your messages penetrate the barrier to reach the people in your audience.

Throughout your talk, take positive steps to overcome this invisible barrier. Make use of all areas of the stage, including the edge. Step off the stage into the area where the people in your audience are seated, if appropriate. There is no rule that dictates that you must stay on the stage. You may move freely, though if you do, make sure the entire audience can still hear and see you.

Some conference facilities don't have a stage or chairs. The speaker stands and the audience stands. Consider how you will use the space so the people in your audience feel 'connected' to you and your presentation.

You are not a recording

One of the great joys of public speaking is that it is live. It is you with a live audience in real time in real life, presenting ideas and gracing people who are genuinely interested in what you have to say with an exclusive opportunity to have a challenging and meaningful exchange with you of the kind that just isn't possible any other way.

You are present. Your audience is present. Everything that takes place happens in the present. When you are truly present you are aware of how the people in your audience are reacting to what you're saying. You will make subtle changes to how you present your ideas on-the-fly in response to shifts in energy in the room. You never 'switch off' or go onto 'auto-pilot'. You remain fully focussed in the present and completely aware of the other people in the room at all times.

GIVE IT A GO! 31
Is she present?

Next time you watch someone speak to an audience observe whether or not you think she is truly 'present'.

Is she 'in the moment' or on 'auto-pilot'?

How does she cope with interruptions?

Does she seem fully connected with the audience?

Is there anything from her performance that you might bring to your own?

Remember to watch the video at www.publicspeakingmojo.co.uk

The creation of presence takes skill, focus and effort. In Chapter 11 we will consider presence in greater depth.

Performance

All public speaking is a performance.

It isn't an act, however. Actors possess an entirely different skillset to public speakers. You may have noticed that many Hollywood actors struggle to communicate clearly during promotional press junkets. This is because they are used to reacting to a script and a director. Without these, most are lost, so much so that those with genuine ability as both actors and speakers tend to stay in your memory (George Clooney or Angelina Jolie, for example).

As I said in Chapter 5, the volume, tone and gestures that you use when speaking to someone one-to-one are insufficient when you are talking to a large group of people. Everything must be turned up a notch (turned up to 'eleven') when you perform to a larger group. Note again that I suggest you turn it up to 'eleven', not to 'twenty'. You do not need to shout at the people in your audience or gesticulate wildly to be heard and understood. Just turn it up one notch higher than you usually would.

When you leave the stage and talk to members of the audience one-to-one, remember to turn your volume back down to 'seven' or 'eight'. 'Eleven' is too much for one-to-one conversation.

GIVE IT A GO! 32
Turning it down

Next time you watch a speaker you enjoy, see if you can grab him for a quick chat after his presentation.

When you do, notice how he adapts his communication style when speaking to you one-to-one.

He is the same person with the same ideas, knowledge and values but his communication style will be more appropriate for a one-to-one conversation.

Remember to watch the video at www.publicspeakingmojo.co.uk

An ability to deal with interruptions successfully

Have you noticed how easy it is to lose your train of thought or your momentum when a noise or other distraction interrupts the attention of the person you are speaking to? It will take the other person a few moments to come back to you and re-focus on what you were saying (they may even say 'I'm sorry, what were you saying?'). It may also take you some time to pick up your thread with the same enthusiasm for what you were saying before you were interrupted.

Imagine how much more severe this problem is for a public speaker. All it takes is for someone to walk in late, banging the door behind them, to shift the focus of the people in the audience from you to the source of the distraction.

Re-focus from distraction

As well as re-focussing yourself you must also re-focus the attention of your audience back to what you were saying quickly so as not to lose precious time. This is precisely why (in Chapter 4) I encourage you to prepare around fifteen percent less material than you need to fill your timeslot. It can take the audience some time to recover from distraction yet the clock continues to tick. It is awful to be told to stop speaking before you have finished so leave space when you prepare your talk to accommodate inevitable interruptions. In a game of football, players get extra time to compensate for interruptions. Sadly, public speakers do not.

How to deal with interruptions successfully:

- Smile and gently but quickly bring the focus back to the presentation

- Don't allow the interruption to be the most interesting part of your talk

- Be patient with interruptions such as chatting in the audience but ask everyone to be quiet if the interruption persists

---

GIVE IT A GO! 33
Dealing with interruptions

Next time you are in an audience and there is some kind of interruption, notice how the speaker deals with it.

Does she ignore it or does she pause while the audience members refocus their attention?

How does she bring the attention of the audience members back to the presentation?

What do you learn from the way other speakers deal with interruptions?

Remember to watch the video at www.publicspeakingmojo.co.uk

The Environment

When invited to speak at an event do you assume the organiser will take care of all of your needs and the needs of the people in your audience? I'm sorry to tell you that almost all of the time, other than promoting the event and collating audience feedback (more about this in Chapter 15) most event organisers do far less to ensure the success of your presentation than you might imagine.

There are many environmental factors that can impact upon the success of your presentation:

↪ Lighting

↪ External noise

↪ Temperature

↪ Air conditioning

↪ Location of toilets

↪ Availability of refreshments

↪ Comfort of chairs

↪ Ability to hear you clearly

↪ Ability to see you clearly

If you have an opportunity to see the space you will be speaking in before the day of your event, do so. You will immediately spot potential problems with the layout of the room. When you enter the room, imagine it from the perspective of your audience and ask yourself how the space should be arranged to give them the best possible experience.

GIVE IT A GO! 34
The right environment

Next time you are an audience member at a conference look around you.

Notice what has been done to make the environment right for you.

What could be done to improve it even more?

Remember to watch the video at www.publicspeakingmojo.co.uk

Chapter Eleven

Charisma, rapport and presence: the building blocks of authentic performance

> ## "Charm is more valuable than beauty. You can resist beauty but you cannot resist charm."
>
> — AUDREY TATOU —

A gift or a skill?

Did you ever watch someone perform on stage and think to yourself 'Wow, I wish I had their charisma'? I bet you have. I bet you also believe their magnetism is 'natural' and there is no way that you could 'learn' how to be charismatic.

I do not believe that charisma, rapport and presence are natural gifts at all. I believe they are skills. And as they are skills you can master them too.

Charisma – what it is, why you want it and how to develop it

I found a lovely definition of 'charisma' in online encyclopaedia Wikipedia:

'Compelling attractiveness or charm that can inspire devotion in others.'

I love the power behind these words: compelling, inspire, devotion. Every public speaker should 'inspire devotion'.

So how can you develop charisma?

1. **Speak passionately**. It is easier to appear charismatic when you seem to really care about what you are talking about. So do not hold back. Put energy into your delivery so that whether or not the people in your audience agree with you they cannot help but feel that you really are committed to your cause. Enthusiasm is infectious.

2. **Use emotive language**. While it is important to speak plainly also speak surprisingly. Resist the temptation to trot out the usual clichés. Instead choose words that give the audience pause for thought.

   Why say "The project went well" when you can say "The project was a phenomenal success, a brilliant plan enacted with courage and flair that delivered incredible results"? None of these words is jargon or requires a high reading age. Even here on the page you can sense the passion behind the words. Strive to make your points with as much energy and emotion as you can muster (without resorting to untruths or wild exaggerations).

3. **Shine a light on other people**. If you are one of several speakers at a conference make a point of paying compliments to the other speakers. It will make you look good (by 'good' I mean generous and selfless!). Include the conference hosts in your praise as well.

   Another group of people to 'shine your light' on are any case study participants whom you mention in your presentation. Be generous in your praise of people whom you admire or who have helped you.

   The third group of people you should shine your light on

is, of course, the people in your audience. Make them feel special. Thank them for bothering to turn up (there are literally a hundred other places they might have chosen to be).

If you want the people in your audience to do something for you remind them of how helpful and wise and good at doing the right thing you know they are and then ask them to do something you 'believe they can' do. This may sound contrived but give it a go and watch what happens. People like to please. Praise your audience and tell them you believe they are capable of doing whatever it is you are asking them to do. You may be pleasantly surprised by the results.

4. **Be charming.** Bring the loveliest version of yourself to the stage. This is one of the reasons why the pre-talk routine that I describe in Chapter 12 is so important. Do not bring frustration or disappointment onto the stage (unless it is by way of illustrating your point). A bad-tempered speaker is excruciating to watch. Instead, adopt the mindset of the most seductive version of yourself. Channel your inner Kylie Minogue or George Clooney. Be smooth and unflappable.

5. **Be inspiring.** It is not sufficient to make your audience feel inspired. You must also inspire them to act! Inspiration without action is pointless. Tell your audience what positive action you would like them to take and encourage them to let you know how they get on in their endeavours. Action that leads to positive change is true inspiration.

6. Make your audience feel something. A presentation isn't just about *what* you say. It is also about how what you say makes your audience feel. You have the ability to make the people in your audience smile with recognition one moment and cry with empathy the next. You can take them on a journey into their own imagination over the course of which they may come to realisations that will change their lives and the lives of those around them forever. For a speaker there is no better feeling than when a member of your audience tells you that you have moved them in some way. It is a privilege to be the person who helps another to realise how they can make a positive difference in the world.

7. Be authentic. Authenticity is just another word for 'real' or 'genuine'. Once the people in your audience believe you are authentic they will more readily accept what you say and will be more eager to do what you ask of them.

Put all seven of these elements together in practice and you will begin to become more charismatic. You may not feel any different right away but listen out for remarks from people who watch you speak. When you start to receive comments such as 'Wow, you really made me think' or 'I would love to support you' you will know your charisma is taking effect.

GIVE IT A GO! 35
With charisma

Next time you give a presentation make a conscious effort to deliver it with as much charisma as you can muster.

Be patient and wait for members of your audience to react to you in increasingly powerful ways (and let me know what happens, please!).

Remember to watch the video at www.publicspeakingmojo.co.uk

Rapport – what it is, why you want it and how to develop it

Oxford Dictionaries offers a definition of rapport that suits public speakers very well:

'A close and harmonious relationship in which the people or groups concerned understand each other's feelings or ideas and communicate well.'

Many people wrongly think rapport means 'agreement', but it doesn't. If you have rapport with someone it means you understand one another. You may also happen to agree but equally you may disagree.

If you come away from a conversation disagreeing with a person but understanding and respecting their point of view then it is safe to say that you have built rapport with them. This is how rapport works in a one-to-one conversation. Can rapport also be established between a speaker and an audience?

Public speakers are not preachers. Rapport – understanding – with your audience really matters. When the people in your audience understand you they will be more likely to act in the way you would like them to. When you understand them, you are more likely to deliver content they appreciate in a style that works.

So how do you build rapport with everyone in your audience?

1. **Open body gestures**. Start to notice what you are doing with your body when you speak. To project well and with positivity, stand symmetrically with your feet planted on the floor hip-width apart. Don't fold your arms or clasp them in front of or behind you, but keep your palms open and remember to allow yourself to use hand gestures that support what you are saying. While it is tempting to hold notes or a slide-clicker, put these to one side when you are not using them so you can use open palm gestures to express yourself.

2. **Head movements**. When saying something with which you would like the people in your audience to agree nod your head. When saying something with which you would like them to disagree shake your head. Notice how they automatically nod or shake their heads when you do. If most of them fail to mirror your head movements then you will know that you have to work a little harder on explaining your point-of-view to them.

3. **Eye contact**. Sweep your gaze across the room during your presentation. Doing so will give everyone the feeling

that you are speaking directly to them. To emphasise a point widen your eyes a little. To invite questioning or agreement, raise your eyebrows and tilt your head.

TIP: You can use eye contact to build rapport with the people in your audience before you have stepped on stage. Make a conscious effort to make eye contact with as many people as you can from the moment you arrive at the venue. On an unconscious level they will believe they already know you. When you step on stage they will already be warm to you.

4. **Smile**. A smile is powerful. When you smile at the people in your audience you show them that, far from being afraid of them, you like them. Your smile will help them to relax and to feel included. Remember to smile when you speak and when you pause. Notice the effect it has on the people in the room.

5. **Lean in.** In conversation, leaning in towards another person creates intimacy. It can also create a sense of conspiracy ('we're in this together'). You can lean in when talking to a large group of people too. Bend forward at the waist slightly and spread your arms, palms facing the people in your audience giving them the feeling that they are being brought into your confidence.

6. **Oral signals.** Your presentation is not only words and gestures. At times you may gasp or exclaim ('Ah', 'Oh', 'Ooh') to emphasise or reflect on a point. Doing so invites the people in your audience to exclaim along with you and to share the sentiment you are expressing. Notice how people respond to your oral signals.

7. Questions and remarks. Rather than delivering a continuous, linear narrative, create powerful pause points during your presentation by asking rhetorical questions and remarking to yourself and the people in your audience on what you just said. Ask of yourself the questions that you have planted in your audience members' minds. If you are not sure what I mean take a look at the structure of any Shakespearian soliloquy, where the actor 'thinks aloud' as a means of delivering a narrative to the audience.

8. Look away. You should look at the people in your audience most of the time. However, by looking away from them from time-to-time you can indicate that you are in deep thought. This can be a very useful device for building rapport as it suggests that you are not simply trotting out a memorised speech, but really thinking about what you are saying. If you appear to be thinking hard, the people in your audience are likely to act on your cue and begin to think hard too.

9. Pause. Few speakers make adequate use of pausing. It's a shame because the simple pause is such a powerful tool for building rapport. A well-placed pause indicates reflection and thought which are key indicators of strong leadership. It takes courage to leave space for silence in a presentation but doing so can give the impression of incredible strength and wisdom. Do not be afraid that your pause will invite heckling. This rarely comes to pass. It is more likely that your pause will either be allowed to resonate or will be filled by encouraging 'oral signals' from the people in your audience.

10. Touch yourself. Want to show the people in your audience that you care? Touch your heart. Want to show them that you are confused, clever or trying to remember something? Touch your head. Gestures do not have to be in the space in front of you. There are plenty of ways you can touch your own body to tell the people in your audience how you are feeling. This type of body movement is known as kinesthesis. When your audience knows how you are feeling you are building rapport.

GIVE IT A GO! 36
Build rapport with someone you don't get on with

Of all the exercises in this book, this one is my favourite.

Think of a person you usually do not get on with. Not someone you actively dislike, but a person with whom you can never seem to find common ground.

Seek them out and do all in your power to build rapport with them. Remember, this is not about agreeing. Your goal is to show the other person that you understand them and to be sure that they understand you.

Give it a go and notice all that happens. Is your relationship with this person any easier after the exercise?

Remember to watch the video at www.publicspeakingmojo.co.uk

Presence – what it is, why you want it and how to develop it

To be present is to experience life right in this moment.

For public speakers, 'presence' is about a lot more than merely turning up. To have presence means to be fully aware of how your presentation is being received by the people in your audience. You are fully awake to their needs and to how effectively you are communicating your ideas to them. And because you are fully awake you are able to alter aspects of your presentation in response to the subtle, verbal or non-verbal feedback you receive from your audience while you are giving your presentation.

From the perspective of the people in your audience, a speaker who has presence is engaging, inspiring and mesmerising. It is very hard to ignore a speaker who has presence. She captivates her audience, enabling them to become fully immersed in what she is saying.

Presence is one of the most difficult skills to master. It requires that you remain fully aware of everything that is happening with you, the room and the people in your audience as you speak. You will keep your self-talk in check. You will notice changes in energy in the room and respond to them appropriately so that your audience will continue to receive the very best experience of your presentation.

A route to developing the skill of presence, one that is fast gaining popularity in Western cultures, is a form of meditation known as 'mindfulness'.

Presence requires true 'mindfulness'

'Mindfulness' is a state of mental awareness and a form of meditation. It is a calm, non-judgmental acknowledgement of what is happening around you. This includes your own thoughts and feelings and the sensations in your body as well as your audience's reaction to you and anything else that might be happening in the room.

As well as helping you to be more aware of your performance and the needs of your audience, mindfulness can also be very useful if you want to hush the sound of your own, intrusive self-talk when you are giving a presentation. When you are in a mindful state, you will notice unwanted thoughts but won't follow them. Instead, you will favour the present by gently acknowledging and then dismissing unwanted thoughts.

Your thoughts are neither 'good' nor 'bad' they are just thoughts. Some thoughts may appear at the wrong time, but this doesn't mean they are 'bad' – they're just in the wrong place. Mindfulness is a really effective technique for dismissing thoughts that you do not want to have 'right now'.

During your presentation there are many things to be mindful of:

⟱ Interruptions that might affect your audience's ability to really hear you

⟱ How well your audience is understanding you

⟱ The clarity with which you are communicating your message

↪ How comfortable your audience is feeling

↪ Your own 'self-talk' and other unwanted or distracting thoughts.

How to be mindful

Mindfulness is a skill and like any skill you must practise it in order to develop your ability to be mindful.

GIVE IT A GO! 37
An introduction to mindfulness

Audio: I have created a one-hour audio presentation that will give you a good introduction to mindfulness for public speakers. The other voice you will hear on the recording is mindfulness meditation trainer Anne Murray.

Listen to it here: www.publicspeakingmojo.co.uk

Remember to watch the video at www.publicspeakingmojo.co.uk

The audio presentation includes a couple of exercises that will help you to discover how to use your thoughts and your breath as a basis for developing the skill of mindfulness.

Once you understand how mindfulness can help you develop your presence as a public speaker, try the following exercise.

GIVE IT A GO! 38
Your five senses

Think about your five senses: sight, hearing, smell, taste and touch.

Now think about how you can ensure that you are using all of your senses during a presentation to keep yourself awake to the present.

What can you see? What sounds can you hear? What can you smell? What is the taste in your mouth? When you touch an object or a part of your body how does it feel?

If you find any of the information that you receive from your senses distracting imagine how distracting it must also be for your audience. Be aware of what is happening around you all the time and be alert to any distractions that you can address.

Remember to watch the video at www.publicspeakingmojo.co.uk

Next time you speak remember to be aware of all the sights, sounds, smells and sensations that you and the people in your audience are experiencing. See what you can do to help your audience to be as present as you are.

GIVE IT A GO! 39
More about mindfulness

Audio: This is a second one-hour audio presentation to help you understand how mindfulness can help you to be a more present public speaker. It includes a couple of visualisation practices. Again, the other voice you will hear on the recording is mindfulness meditation trainer Anne Murray.

Listen to it here: www.publicspeakingmojo.co.uk

Remember to watch the video at www.publicspeakingmojo.co.uk

Using mindfulness to write your presentation

You now know how to use mindfulness during your presentation to ensure that you are fully present to the needs of your audience. In Chapter 12 I will tell you how you can use mindfulness as part of a pre-talk routine to get yourself into the right mindset for giving a successful presentation. You may also find it useful to practise mindfulness when you are deciding what to put in your presentation.

I have not mentioned the content of your presentation in this book because there are many other excellent books available to help you put a fascinating and high-impact talk together ('How to be Brilliant at Public Speaking' by Sarah Lloyd-Hughes is a wonderful example). However, you might find it useful to know a little more about how I put a presentation together using mindfulness meditation.

I have never sat down at a computer to write a presentation. In fact, I find nothing less creatively simulating than a computer screen! By the time I get to the computer the entire presentation is already mapped out in my mind, including what I am going to say and how I am going to say it, my 'calls to action' and any stories that I will use to illustrate my main points. I believe this happens at least in part because I have formed a habit of practising mindfulness meditation daily.

I use mindfulness meditation at the start of my day to find some mental calm. However, I also practise mindfulness when I'm walking and when I'm listening to music, in particular, music that enables me to experience 'theta' brain waves

Brain waves that occur at frequencies of four to seven cycles per second are known as 'theta' brainwaves. Theta brainwaves are associated with 'right-brain thinking' and it is believed that when you are in this mind state you can have greater access to creative thinking and the contents of your unconscious mind. If this is of interest to you I have listed a useful book on the subject of theta brain waves and creativity in the bibliography at the end of this book.

(Note that you will easily find recordings of 'brain wave entrainment music' on YouTube. These are designed to take you into a state of deep trance. If you decide to use them do not listen to them when driving or doing any activity that requires that you be alert.)

Where do creative ideas come from?

Have you ever noticed that great ideas or the solutions to problems that have been taxing you for some time seem to come to you when you are not trying to think about them, such as when you are in the shower or driving your car? Research by neuroscientists has recently found that we can often access a more creative state of mind when we stop focussing on a problem.

When we stop thinking about a problem we free our minds to go searching through the knowledge we store in the unconscious part of our brain.

Rather than trying to think of great ideas for your presentations, create conditions where you brain can be left to discover great ideas for you. Go for a walk, go for a drive, have a shower! If this is of interest to you I have listed a couple of useful articles on the subject of the creative mind in the bibliography at the end of this book.

Mindfulness is one way of coming up with ideas for your presentations, but there are many more.

Just like the comedians

Think about an observational comedian, such as Lee Evans, Sarah Millican or Michael McIntyre (search for them on YouTube if you haven't come across them before). They have all achieved mass appeal because they are extremely adept at noticing life's small details. When constructing your talk consider how you can include observations that will make the people in your audience smile (or reflect) with recognition. It is not necessary to crack jokes to make your audience warm to you. Talk about the familiar things everyone can relate to.

Always carry a notebook

As inspiration can strike at any time, carry a notebook (or note-taking device) wherever you go. Ideas can disappear as quickly as they arrive. There is nothing more infuriating than to have a brilliant idea one moment and forget it the next.

If a great idea comes to you during meditation, break from your meditation and write it down. Do not let good ideas get away from you! Return to your meditative state once you have noted the good idea.

GIVE IT A GO! 40
Take notes

Make a habit of noting down instances from your daily life that serve to illustrate key messages in your talk.

Be creative. Make connections between things that are mundane-but-relatable and your main points.

Remember to watch the video at www.publicspeakingmojo.co.uk

Emotion and authenticity

People love to be taken on an emotional journey. This is why story-telling is such an effective teaching device. To be truly authentic, bring some of your own emotion to your presentation. For many speakers this is a horrifying thought, particularly if you have been hiding behind the invisible barrier that exists between you and the people in your audience. In British culture, we are not encouraged to express how we feel in front of strangers. As children we may even have been punished for showing 'too much' emotion. The thought of 'opening up' to a group of strangers may be horrifying. However, if you can learn to do it your openness will be rewarded.

If you can make an audience laugh or cry, feel anger, outrage or sympathy then you have created true rapport with them. It is possible to do this without sharing any of your own emotion or experiences, but it is more difficult. Experiment with bringing as much emotion and passion to the stage as you dare. You may find this difficult at first but remember this is not about sharing personal secrets or things about yourself that you feel uncomfortable talking about in public. Rather, you are seeking to give the people in the audience a 'that could happen to me too' feeling. Start tentatively and find the level of candour at which you and they feel comfortable.

If you can show vulnerability by taking a step or two beyond what you are usually comfortable talking about you may find that the people in your audience will respond very positively. People like the feeling of 'me too'. We are social creatures who feel reassured when we encounter someone who has the same emotional reaction to life events that we do. The trouble is, our fear of being rejected for our honesty is very powerful! If you can find the courage to share something personal about yourself despite the associated risks you may be delighted by how your audience responds to you.

GIVE IT A GO! 41
It's emotional

Next time you put a presentation together consider how you can deliver it with maximum emotion.

What genuine emotion can you bring to the stage that will help your audience to appreciate the importance of your words?

Remember to watch the video at www.publicspeakingmojo.co.uk

Come out from behind the lectern

It can be tempting to stand behind a lectern when you speak. It gives you something to hold onto and a sense of security and stability (mentally and physically). However, when you stand behind a lectern the people in your audience cannot see most of your body. This may not seem particularly important to you but you will be amazed how much it matters to them.

A key aspect of 'presence' is openness. You can be open

in what you say (how much you share and with whom and in the accessibility of your language). You can also be open with your body. However, when you stand behind a lectern you mask two-thirds of your body. Without meaning to, this creates a disconnection between you and the people in the audience who are prevented from seeing your 'whole body' communicate. Without realising, you are using the lectern as a barrier and barriers interrupt the flow of communication.

By standing in the middle of the platform (as TED Talk speakers are required to do www.TED.com) you present a much more open, more authentic, less threatening and less 'suspicious' body image to your audience.

GIVE IT A GO! 42
In full view

When you next speak in front of an audience stand in full view away from the lectern.

Notice how your audience reacts to you.

Warning: always check that your audience can hear you if you move away from the lectern microphone. Remember that some members of the audience may be hard-of-hearing and rely on the 'loop' system to hear you. Ideally, you should use a lapel microphone.

Remember to watch the video at www.publicspeakingmojo.co.uk

By standing symmetrically, face-on with your audience and with your whole body in view you send a message to them that you are not afraid of them and that you are open and can be trusted. This is very powerful. Imagine trying to convey all of this with words. It would take some time to convince a room of people that you can be trusted. Yet with an open posture you immediately begin to break down the invisible barriers.

TIP: Take a tip from your cat! When a cat has grown to trust its owner it will lie on its back with its tummy exposed to you. Its tummy is the cat's most sensitive area. Your cat definitely does not want you to touch its tummy and under no circumstances should you try! By showing you its most vulnerable part your cat is letting you know how much he trusts you. Apply 'cat logic' to the people in your audience. Show them you trust them by letting them see your entire body. Don't hide it behind a lectern!

Chapter Twelve

Perfect practice: how to rehearse the right way

> # "Practice does not make perfect. Only perfect practice makes perfect."
> — VINCE LOMBARDI —

The big secret

Have you noticed that some public speakers are never lost for words no matter how deep the crisis? From failed equipment to noisy interruptions nothing seems to faze them. So what's their secret? What do they do that sets them apart from the speakers who panic and dry up when something unexpected happens?

The 'big secret' is practice. However, it's a very particular kind of practice; a kind that makes the most of your brain's love of learning.

Think about a time when you learned a new skill, such as driving. At first, it took you a while to get the hang of all the actions you need to take to get the car moving. After a few lessons you found that you could start the car, put it into the correct gear and drive away smoothly without thinking about it too much. It was almost as if you could drive 'automatically'.

If you don't drive, perhaps you have learned to play a sport or a musical instrument. Or maybe your job requires that you master a piece of complex machinery. You found the task difficult at first, but by attempting it repeatedly you were eventually able to do it really well without too much conscious effort.

Your brain loves to learn

There is nothing your brain loves more than to learn something new and it learns through practice.

Every task you perform is comprised of a sequence of actions. Each time you perform the actions your brain commits the sequence to memory. Every time you repeat the sequence (i.e. practise) your brain makes the connections between the actions in the sequence stronger and stronger. Over time, your brain is able to recall the sequence very quickly, so quickly that the process feels automatic.

To feel more confident about your presentation practise again and again and again. With each practice your brain will make the connections between the component parts of your presentation stronger and easier to recall without requiring you to think too hard.

Processing power

Practising has other benefits. When your brain has learned key elements of your presentation it needs to do a lot less 'processing' (conscious thinking) when you repeat the task. This is fantastic news for public speakers. With much of your conscious brain freed up, you can turn your focus on other elements of your presentation, such as ad-libbing, dealing with interruptions or problems and other aspects of presence.

Practise, don't memorise

It is a mistake to try to memorise you presentation word-for-word. Great presentations are not great because they are word perfect. Great presentations are great because they are delivered with passion and authenticity by a speaker who really cares about the impact of his or her message. If you attempt to recite your presentation word-for-word from memory what happens if you stumble on a word? The concentration of the people in your audience will be broken while you scramble to get back on track. Unless you happen to be a trained actor, a memorised speech will always sound contrived and feel inauthentic.

Contrast a memorised speech with a rehearsed presentation and the difference from the audience's perspective is like night versus day. A well-rehearsed performance may not be word perfect, but it will be more authentic and authenticity is the mark of phenomenal, memorable performance.

Mental rehearsal (with a twist)

You may have already heard about a technique known as 'mental rehearsal'. As the name suggests, during a mental rehearsal you visualise (imagine in your mind) yourself performing your presentation for real.

The premise is very simple. If you visualise yourself performing well as you rehearse your unconscious mind will commit to memory the feelings associated with your rehearsal performances. When you perform for real, your unconscious mind will recall your mental rehearsals and you'll feel just as good when you perform in front of an audience as you did in your rehearsals.

The mental rehearsal technique that I would like you to practise has an important twist as it combines visualisation with physical performance.

When you rehearse, let go of the need to be one hundred per cent word perfect. Getting your words in the right order is not what matters to the people in your audience. What they care about (whether they are aware of it or not) is how well you communicate with them and how authentic you appear to be.

Rehearse your presentation by yourself in real time. There are so many benefits to rehearsing this way. When you are alone you don't have to worry over what anyone else thinks. You can be fully focused on your performance, concentrating on how your performance feels rather than what it looks like.

The very first time you rehearse in this way you will immediately become aware of how your presentation flows. It is very likely that in the time between your first and second rehearsals you will make many adjustments to your presentation to enable it to flow more smoothly.

Rehearsing in real time helps you to become aware of the length of your presentation. By setting a timer you will know whether the presentation you have planned is too long or too short. If you finish a rehearsal before your timer beeps then you know your presentation is the right length. If your timer beeps and you have yet to finish your presentation reduce the content by ten percent and rehearse again.

Mental Rehearsal – step-by-step

What to do	What you will notice
1. Rehearse your presentation by yourself in real time	• You will feel how your presentation flows • You will know if it is too long or too short
2. Perform with as much charisma, rapport and presence as you can muster	• Really give it your all and when you do it for real your audience will get so much more
3. Practise this way as many times as you can before the day of your real performance	• Every time you rehearse your clever brain will store elements of your performance in your unconscious mind for easy access next time you perform your presentation
4. Never rehearse in front of a mirror or an audience	• If you catch sight of yourself in a mirror you are giving that dissenting voice in your head an opportunity to undermine your confidence. Don't let it! • Your family and friends are not your audience. Their opinions do not count!
5. As you rehearse, visualise yourself doing brilliantly	• Notice how good you are feeling and that you keep feeling better with each rehearsal
6. When you visualise your audience, be compassionate!	• No one taught an audience how to behave. Be prepared that they may look tired and disconnected. If they do, have compassion and turn your charisma, rapport and presence volume up to eleven!

When you rehearse, give your performance all you have got in terms of charisma, rapport and presence. Turn your volume up to 'eleven'. Immerse yourself in your performance. The more often you rehearse in this way, the more confident you will feel. You will notice a pleasurable rush of endorphins when a rehearsal goes well and when you feel your performance is improving you will become excited at the prospect of giving your presentation for real.

Remember that family feedback and mirrors are bad for your rehearsal. Mental rehearsal is all about the way you feel, not the way you look to other people. Stay strong and never let anyone but your intended audience see your rehearsals. Do not let your friends or family or your own reflection take your mojo away!

This kind of mental rehearsal, that combines visualisation with performance, is the most helpful public speaking preparation technique I have ever come across. If you commit to doing regular mental rehearsals in the days running up to your presentation the quality of your performance on the day will amaze you.

You may be wondering why, if the technique is so helpful and so simple, so few people do it. I believe the answer lies in commitment. Most people are not committed to doing what it takes to ensure their performance is great. Most people prefer to not think about their performance until the night before they are due to do it. Most people think rehearsals are boring and unnecessary. Most people are destined to be mediocre public speakers, unfortunately.

The one big difference between mediocre speakers and brilliant speakers is the mental rehearsal. Practise regularly and your clever brain will do the rest. If you find rehearsals boring remind yourself of how wonderful you will feel when you perform your presentation for real. You will feel so confident that you will be able to deal with anything.

Do not take my word for it. Give it a go yourself. Get into the habit of doing mental rehearsals in the days leading up to every presentation that you give. You will be amazed by the results.

GIVE IT A GO!
43 Mental rehearsal

In the days leading up to the day of your presentation make time to perform at least two full mental rehearsals per day.

Set a timer and no matter what happens while you are rehearsing keep going.

With every rehearsal you will notice your performance becomes easier, smoother and more enjoyable.

Remember to watch the video at www.publicspeakingmojo.co.uk

The value of a pre-talk routine

Mental rehearsals are of great help in the days leading up to your presentation, but you may wonder what you can do to put yourself into the right mindset in the moments before you give your presentation.

In Chapter 9, I explained how you can manage your adrenalin, cortisol and testosterone effectively. What you learned about power posing can be an effective part of your pre-talk routine. Add to this a few techniques to 'warm up' your voice and your body and you will be as ready to give a great presentation as Usain Bolt when he prepares to run the 100 metres.

How to create your own pre-talk routine

Your pre-talk routine can be whatever you want it to be. It works best when you can perform it anywhere. Avoid relying on lucky mascots or a particular pair of shoes or anything you might forget to take with you to the venue.

The simplest and best routines are ones that you can perform in just a few minutes. When you arrive at the venue find yourself a quiet room where you can perform your routine without being disturbed. If there is no private room available find a toilet cubicle!

Your pre-talk routine may include any of the following:

Power pose

In Chapter 9 you learned that in just two minutes you can increase your body's testosterone levels and become happier, more confident and less inhibited. Remember: TWO MINUTES!

Deep breathing

With your eyes closed take a number of slow, deep breaths through your nose down into your body. Notice that the air is cool as it comes into your body and warmer as it leaves your body. If you like, you can imagine breathing in confidence and success and breathing out stress and self-doubt.

Visualisation

Think back to your recent mental rehearsals and recall how good they felt. Visualise yourself performing for real. Notice how much you enjoy it and how well you are doing.

I find it helpful to focus on a particular word or emotion in the minutes before I step on stage, such as 'peace', 'energy', 'love' or 'power'.

Vocal warm-up

Take a slow deep breath and hum until you can exhale no more. Do this four times. Repeat, but this time open your mouth part way through each hum so the sound changes from 'Mmm' to 'Ahh'. Practise a few tongue-twisters such as 'unique New York' and 'Sheila needs, Sheila leads'.

Stretch

Following your power pose reach up above your head and stretch. You may also like to stretch some of the muscles in your legs.

Drink water

Even if you don't feel thirsty, drink water. Speaking dehydrates your body so take a few gulps of water before you take to the stage. Notice if there is air conditioning in the room you will be speaking in. Aircon is notorious for drying out vocal cords. Ask the venue organiser if the aircon can be switched off for the duration of your talk (he will probably say 'No') and make sure you have a glass of water to hand at all times. Your voice needs water.

You may be thinking that a pre-talk routine is yet more work on top of everything else you need to think about. It is, but if you take your performance seriously and want to do the best job that you possibly can a pre-talk routine is really important because it will help you to get you into the right mindset for giving a great performance.

Take preparation really seriously every single time you make a presentation, even when you do not feel that you need to. Pre-talk routines work because they can be used as triggers to alert your brain and body to get ready to give a great performance.

Call upon the professional you

While I strongly discourage you from dissociating from the 'present', if you feel uncomfortable as you step on stage imagine that you are in a situation that requires you to be your most professional self. Be the person who you are at work: confident, knowledgeable, experienced and in control.

Tip: If you are asked to speak at a funeral but worried that you may not be able to keep your emotions under control try becoming your most professional self. While friends and family may try to reassure you that tears are okay they really are not okay if they prevent you from speaking! (This book's 'Afterword' includes a case study about one of my clients who used the 'professional self' technique to speak at a funeral with great success.)

A note about notes

Just before you step on stage re-familiarise yourself with the notes that you have made about your talk. Your notes should be in the form of succinct bullet points. Do not write long paragraphs of text. When you are performing your presentation you will be able to read bullet points far more easily than blocks of text. Think of your notes as a prompt rather than a script.

The stand-up comedian Stewart Lee writes his bullet points on his hand. If you are able to catch sight of these notes during one of his televised performances you will notice that each bullet point is one word that represents a section of his routine. If you have been practising your mental rehearsals regularly you should find that one-word bullet points are all you need too. Remember that you are performing not reciting.

GIVE IT A GO! 44
From notes

Using a presentation you have given previously, reduce the content down to note form. Then down to bullet point form. Then to just one word per idea

Now rehearse that presentation a few times using the list of single words.

What do you notice each time you rehearse?

Does your performance become smoother and more natural?

Remember to watch the video at www.publicspeakingmojo.co.uk

Chapter Thirteen

Stop your rambling for good

> # "Too much glue won't stick, and too many words won't either."
>
> — ANONYMOUS —

If you know you ramble, you are not alone. Many of the people who look at my website arrive there after searching Google for advice on how to stop rambling. I have to confess, I used to be a terrible rambler too.

There are two main types of rambler.

Type 1: ramble because they are ill-prepared.

Type 2: ramble because they enjoy the sound of their own voice a little too much.

Which one are you?

What is rambling?

Rambling is 'speaking without purpose'.

You may ramble for any number of reasons:

⚡ Nerves may cause you to lose your train of thought so you just keep on talking in the hope the train will come back to you.

⚡ You don't want to lose control of 'the floor'.

Politicians are frequent ramblers. In politics, keeping control of a debate is very important as it prevents the opposition from having their say. Listen to Parliamentary debates and you will hear some MPs rambling on and on in a deliberate attempt to spoil a debate (the parliamentary term for it is 'filibustering'!).

You may ramble because you associate speaking with control. However, if what you are saying is without purpose no one will listen.

↪ You began to speak before you knew what your point was or how you were going to express it.

↪ You began to speak and knew what you were going to say, but, as you were talking, a voice in your own mind (self-talk) distracted you.

↪ You have made the same presentation many times before. After you began to speak you got confused about where you were in your presentation because you were overwhelmed by a sense of déjà vu.

↪ You started speaking and all was going well until someone in the audience gave you a disparaging look. A voice in your head (self-talk again) told you 'this woman doesn't like you' and you chose to believe it. This is where it all fell apart and you lost your place so you rambled in an attempt to find your way back to the point you had been making.

GIVE IT A GO! 45
What type of rambler are you?

Spend a few minutes reading through the list of reasons why people ramble and decide which type of rambler you are.

Does this give you greater insight into why you ramble?

Remember to watch the video at www.publicspeakingmojo.co.uk

Why rambling is a serious matter

When addressing an audience every word you use can have a powerful effect on the people listening to you. Your words can, literally, change people's minds. Talk too much, however, and your message may become diluted. If your message becomes lost in a sea of words you might as well have said nothing at all.

How can you avoid rambling?

It may be that you ramble for several reasons. That's okay, because there is a solution for every type of ramble you can think of.

You lost your train of thought due to nerves

If nerves are getting the better of you refer back to what you have learned about the importance of staying in the present (Chapter 11). Notice when your thoughts are straying from the subject of your presentation. Acknowledge your unwanted thoughts and bring your focus back to the present. If you need to pause then do so. Perhaps take a sip of water and then come back to where you were when you lost your place.

You didn't want to give up the microphone

If you are in the audience and making a point or asking a question during another speaker's question and answer session make your point then stop talking (the same applies if you are one of the speakers in a panel debate). If you make your point in a clear and concise way then there is no need to continue speaking. Before you speak think carefully about how you can make your point with maximum clarity and memorability. It is never about how much you say. It's always about *how* you say it.

You spoke without first thinking it through

In your mind, 'control' may be related to taking the power of being heard away from someone else which is why you sometimes start speaking before you are ready (so you can prevent someone else from having their say). It is always a smart idea to think about how you are going to make your point before you make it so that your message is clear. If that means allowing someone else to beat you to the microphone, then so be it. Rambling is never clear and puts the onus on the listener to work out what your point is.

Self-talk distracted you

In Chapter 11 you learned how to use mindfulness to bring your thoughts back to what is happening now. When you recognise that you are listening to your own self-talk during a presentation gently bring your attention back to the present.

Déjà vu distracted you

When you experience the feeling that you are repeating yourself remember that repetition helps an audience to 'hear' your message. If you feel yourself becoming flustered go back to a slightly earlier point in your talk and continue from there. By preparing to speak for less time than you have been given you can be safe in the knowledge that you have enough time to back-track a little if required.

Someone in the audience distracted you

Notice that you are distracted and bring your attention back to the present. The people in the audience don't usually mean to distract you. Remember this as you notice the distraction and gently bring yourself back to now.

How to speak 'off-the-cuff' without rambling

This section could also be called 'how to be spontaneous'. Have you ever watched someone apparently 'improvise' a presentation and been impressed by their ability to speak with no preparation at all? Improvisation is an illusion. The reason some people appear to be able to speak spontaneously with little effort and few mistakes is because they prepare. It is very

easy to 'improvise' when you have rehearsed how you intend
to express your point many times over.

GIVE IT A GO! 46
Thinking it through

Before attending a meeting or event where you know you
may have an opportunity to speak 'off-the-cuff' set aside
some time to think about the message you intend to put
across.

When you are sure of what your message is jot it down
in a notebook.

Now look at your message and ask yourself 'how can I
say this with the greatest possible impact in the fewest
possible words?'

Re-write your message using high-impact, memorable
language, taking care to put your message across as
succinctly (in as few words) as possible.

Rehearse, either out loud or in your mind. When you are
happy that your message sounds the way you want it to
rehearse it a few more times and jot down the final
wording that you have chosen in your notebook.

When you arrive at the meeting or event take another
look at your notebook to remind yourself of how you are
going to express your message.

When the opportunity comes say what you have planned
to say in the way you have planned to say it and no more.

Resist the temptation to 'hold the floor' and sit back down when you have said what you have intended to say. You have just been eloquent and to-the-point. It makes no sense to dilute your message by out-staying your welcome!

Remember to watch the video at www.publicspeakingmojo.co.uk

It is a very good idea to practise this exercise as a matter of routine even if you have no speaking opportunity coming up. If you are well-practised then you will be able to make the most of unexpected opportunities to speak in future.

Think like a politician. Politicians have the 'party line' drummed into them by their party communications team. Be your own communications advisor and drum your own messages into your mind by rehearsing them often.

'So I won't ramble, but how do I avoid drying up?'

Drying up (being unable to think of the next thing to say) sounds like the opposite of rambling. In fact both rambling and drying up have the same root cause: lack of preparation.

Remember that your brain loves to learn and it learns through practice. When you commit to regular practice using the mental rehearsal technique described in Chapter 12, you will find that your mind 'goes blank' less and less frequently. You may occasionally lose your train of thought but you now know the measures you can take to find it again.

Chapter Fourteen

The glorious climax: why the Q&A is your opportunity to sparkle

> ## "Who questions much, shall learn much, and retain much."
>
> — FRANCIS BACON —

Remind yourself why you speak in public

The goal of all public speaking is to sell something, be it a product, a service or an idea. You speak to draw attention to your product, service or idea and to start a dialogue with people who might be interested in buying or supporting what you're 'selling'. This is why the Q&A (question and answer) section of your talk is just as important as the talk itself. The Q&A is your first opportunity to open a dialogue with individual customers.

The Q&A is a further opportunity for you to sparkle, a chance to show that you know even more about your subject than you shared through your talk. Yet many public speakers say the Q&A is the part of the presentation they dread the most. This is due to the same fear about being judged or being wrong that we covered in Chapter 8. You may be afraid that during the Q&A you will somehow be exposed as a 'fraud', criticised, corrected and humiliated for not knowing everything or getting something wrong. These are disempowering thoughts and it is helpful to challenge them.

Fear of judgement/not having all the answers

If you believe that in order to be a public speaker you have to know everything about everything then it is no surprise that the Q&A makes you feel anxious. The truth is no one knows everything. Even when all the facts are available people can still have differences of opinion about the best way to approach something.

Even subject specialists don't know it all. If you have ever watched the BBC TV quiz show Mastermind then you will know that it is rare for any contestant to score one hundred percent when questioned on their chosen specialised subject. There is no shame in not getting every question right on national television so why allow yourself to feel shame if someone else knows more about an aspect of your subject area than you do?

Apart from feeling embarrassed, what can you do if asked a question you don't know the answer to?

GIVE IT A GO! 47
Throw it out

If you are caught out by a question you can't answer throw it out to the audience. There is a good chance that one of these clever people will be able to answer it for you.

This is not a show of weakness on your part. It's a show of strength.

Confident people don't need to have all the answers. Confident people are honest and open about what they know and what they do not know and are willing to ask for help when they need it.

What's more, when you ask the audience to help with the answer to a question you are inviting them to share your limelight and this will make them feel even warmer towards you.

Remember to watch the video at www.publicspeakingmojo.co.uk

Fear of being 'told off' for getting something wrong

When you were at school there may have been a certain amount of shame attached to getting something wrong in class. Fortunately, 'mistakes' are now considered to be a valuable part of the learning process. However, the sting of embarrassment and fear that you will be chastised in front of other people if you get something wrong can stay with you into adulthood.

If a member of the audience takes it upon themselves to correct an inaccuracy in your presentation in front of the rest of your audience the best way to respond is with gracious compassion. By saying "Thank you" and "I will look into that further" you have successfully diffused the situation, with both parties coming out on top. There is no need for an argument between you and the person who is pointing out the error. If they will not let the matter go tell them you will be really pleased to discuss it 'afterwards' and move on to the next question.

Be the last to leave

Once the Q&A is finished and you have taken your applause should you leave or should you stick around for more?

It is very likely that several people will appreciate the opportunity to speak with you one-to-one before you leave. A face-to-face conversation with someone who might later become a customer or supporter is invaluable. Here is a golden opportunity to build rapport with your new supporters, so do not miss the opportunity to talk to them one-to-one.

If you can, stay at the event until the very end. Treat everyone who approaches you as if they are the most valuable business lead of the day because you never know, they just might be.

GIVE IT A GO! 48
Make them feel important

If someone, or a queue of people, is anxious to speak to you after your presentation, do all in your power to make them feel important.

For instance, find a couple of chairs and invite them to sit down so you can talk to them on the same level.

If they want to compliment you, accept the praise with good grace. Remember that most people have a great deal of respect for public speakers because most people are afraid of public speaking. You have earned their respect, so enjoy it!

Remember to watch the video at www.publicspeakingmojo.co.uk

When you talk to someone after your presentation don't allow the conversation to be all about you. Listen, and don't say too much (your time for speech-making is over!). Take their business card and add them as a LinkedIn connection so you do not lose touch. Direct them to your website and encourage them to email you if they have further thoughts or questions.

TIP: I no longer carry business cards. Instead, I aim to be memorable (it is easy enough to work out how to contact me via the web!). However, I do take other people's business cards. When I return to the office I make sure that I email everyone I met to keep the conversation open, even if it is just to say 'lovely to meet you today'.

Never take any member of your audience for granted. Without them public speaking cannot exist.

Chapter Fifteen

Never read your own reviews: a smarter way to gather feedback

> ## "I have forgotten most of my rave reviews and memorised my vicious ones."
>
> — ERICA JONG —

Don't read your reviews. You may believe them.

There is an evil that can harm any public speaker's self-esteem.

It is, of course, the notorious feedback form.

Let's contemplate the feedback form as if it were an unwanted thought and make it go away!

If it moves measure it

I am old enough to remember when feedback forms were different. They were not handed out during the event, but were posted to delegates several days hence. This was good, because by the time they received the feedback request delegates had had time to reflect on the value of the event. These days, delegates aren't allowed to leave the room until they have provided written feedback. What kind of feedback do you imagine they supply under such duress?

The feedback form has changed in nature as marketing's obsession with measurement has taken hold. Conference delegates are now asked to give everything imaginable a mark out of ten. Unfortunately, speakers are subjected to the same scrutiny as the quality of the coffee and the convenience of the parking. I have seen fantastic speakers reduced to tears over their aggregated feedback mark or harsh comments scribbled in haste.

I have never cried over a feedback form, but I have laughed over a few because this means of assessment has become arbitrary and faintly ridiculous. As a campaigning speaker I don't seek to make the people in the audience like me. I don't seek to make them to approve of me either. And I certainly don't seek their agreement with everything I say. In fact, many people who hear me speak for the first time find me offensive. And so I would hope, because if they agreed with me on first hearing I would be preaching to the converted and that would be no good at all. My goal is to inform and to challenge. Marketers don't seem interested in gathering the kind of feedback that would be useful to me.

I do not believe feedback forms help you. In my experience, people in your audience don't know how they feel about you in the moments immediately after your talk. They need time to assimilate what you have said and to consider how it applies in their lives. This thought process takes time.

A better way to measure

I never read feedback forms and I do not believe you should either. What began life as a means of rating the practical aspects of an event has mutated into a monster that threatens to destroy the self-esteem of perfectly good speakers. Feel free to join my revolution and refuse to have anything to do with them!

GIVE IT A GO! 49
Refuse to read feedback!

You don't have to read these feedback forms.

The next time a conference organiser emails you the collated feedback from your presentation delete the email without opening it!

Note the impact not reading these forms has on your self-esteem.

Remember to watch the video at www.publicspeakingmojo.co.uk

We speak to initiate a dialogue. Experiment with asking your audience what they thought of your presentation at least a week after the event and don't ask them the usual bland questions. Instead, ask questions that will provoke an interesting and useful response.

Questions that I ask delegates of my workshops include:

⚐ What did you learn that surprised you?

⚐ What did you learn that you will apply in your own life?

⚐ How would you describe the workshop to someone else?

Do you see how asking the right questions will solicit feedback that is of far greater use to you?

GIVE IT A GO! 50
Wait!

Resist the temptation to ask for feedback right away.

Wait a few days and ask your audience to provide feedback to you directly via email or over the phone.

You will receive less quantitative feedback, but what you discover will be much more useful to you.

Remember to watch the video at www.publicspeakingmojo.co.uk

The long game

People will not necessarily act on your 'calls to action' immediately, perhaps because they do not yet have the authority to do so. Be patient. When you meet again later in life you may be amazed to discover what your audience members have done with what they learned from you.

Case study: You never know

One of Britain's best known financial services companies re-designed its website to make it more accessible to blind and partially sighted people.

It was some years after this work had been completed that I met the senior manager who had overseen the work (in fact, he'd been the driving force that made it happen).

He told me that it was after seeing one of my presentations some years previously that he had decided that he would do all in his power to make the company's website more accessible to disabled people.

I remember the presentation he refers to but I don't remember him being there.

What lessons can be learned from my experience?

Be patient, because change can take time but is worth the wait.

Always give your best performance as you never know who is listening.

Chapter Sixteen

Checklist for success: revive your mojo now!

> # "There are seven days in the week and someday isn't one of them."
>
> — ANONYMOUS —

In a rush?

If you have a presentation coming up very soon and don't have time to work your way through this book from start to finish then this chapter contains all the shortcuts you need.

Accept responsibility now

I know. It is easier to blame external forces when things go wrong than it is to accept the responsibility. But it is only when you take full responsibility for every aspect of your presentation's success that you give yourself the greatest opportunity of success.

Here are eight final thoughts to set you on your way.

1. Know your audience

Power

Ask your event host to tell you everything they can about your expected audience. How many people do they expect will attend? What is their level of expertise and, more importantly, how much decision-making or purchasing-power do they have? It is no good talking about budgetary issues to people who have no budgetary control. As every presentation you give should climax in a 'call to action' it is vital that you know how much power the people in your audience have so you give them a 'call to action' that they can achieve.

Journalists

If you are speaking at a conference be aware that there may be journalists in the room (whether they have been invited or not!). If you are not happy for it to appear in the media, do not say it! This rule-of-thumb will spare you a lot of embarrassment one day. If you spot a member of the press in your audience, do not let them leave without speaking to them. Many freelancers write stories that are syndicated around the world! Help them to write a great piece about your presentation.

Social media

Be aware that everyone in the audience now has the ability to be a 'citizen journalist' thanks to their mobile phone (or other web-enabled device). Anyone can 'tweet' to the social network Twitter and this can be either a blessing or a curse. It is wonderful that a moment-to-moment account of your presentation can be shared with the world while you are speaking. Unfortunately, few people have either the listening or the editorial skills to tweet fairly or accurately and as you are busy speaking you are unable to monitor audience tweets for quality.

You will never be able to prevent your audience tweeting. They cannot help themselves and see no wrong in what they are doing. So try this trick. At the beginning of your talk, mention that there is a 'hashtag' (a label: '#') for your presentation and encourage people to tweet using that hashtag (for example '#usabconf16' if you are at a conference about usability in 2016). This has two benefits. Once you have left the stage you can search for the hashtag on Twitter and retrieve a list of all the tweets about your presentation. In addition, knowing that you will read their tweets later may make the people in the audience a little more careful about what they tweet.

2. Know your length

Ask the conference organiser how long your presentation should be and prepare to give a presentation of that length minus ten-fifteen per cent. You should always under-run and always leave space for questions. Give yourself some wriggle-room in case of late starts or interruptions. Never be tempted to 'wing it' or to cram all you know into whatever time you have. That is a recipe for an unstructured, unfocussed presentation.

3. Know your point

You speak for one of two reasons: to inform or to persuade/sell. You do not speak for the sake of speaking. Decide what your main point will be and come up with a 'call to action' that your audience will find inspiring and achievable. It is better to limit yourself to three points made well than twenty made badly.

4. Know your venue

Few people check out the conference venue before the day of their presentation. Unless you are already familiar with a particular space there are bound to be crucial differences in the layout that you are not expecting. If you cannot visit the venue before the date of your presentation then ask the conference organiser the following questions:

↝ Is there a platform?

↝ Will I be speaking behind a lectern?

↝ What kind of microphone will I have?

↝ Will there be any disabled people in the audience for whom I should adapt my presentation or materials?

↝ Will the induction loop (for people who are hard of hearing) be in use?

↝ Which floor is the room on and does it have windows (most conference rooms are in a windowless basement)?

Ask as many questions as you can to help you create a vivid mental picture of the space. Doing so will reduce the chances of unwelcome surprises. Check out the venue's website as there may be photographs of the conference space there.

5. Know your format

If there are other speakers on the programme find out who they are and what they will be talking about. Check to see if there are any videos of them speaking online (on

YouTube, for example). This will help you to develop a sense of how they speak so that you can be sure to offer some light or shade to the programme.

If you are speaking after someone who is quite subdued and serious, perhaps this would be a good opportunity for you to be particularly enlivening and upbeat. If the person speaking before you is light-hearted and charismatic, think about what you can do to maintain the high energy of their performance.

Find out whether you will be expected to take questions at the end of your session or whether you will be asked to join a panel for questions at the end of the conference. I counsel against taking questions during your presentation unless you are particularly adept at dealing with interruptions and keeping to time.

6. Know your technology

If you plan to use presentation slides be certain that your technology is compatible with the conference centre's technology. This advice also applies to the humble paper flipchart. I have seen a speaker go into meltdown when he arrived at the conference venue with his entire presentation on flipchart sheets only to discover that there was no flipchart stand available. This stress could have been avoided. Never assume anything.

7. Be a diva

It is vital that you find a few minutes and a quiet space to get into your public speaking mindset by practising your pre-talk routine (see Chapter 12). Be a diva and insist you have this time alone to prepare. The conference organisers want the best from you so make sure they get it by insisting that you have the time and space you need to get yourself 'in the zone'.

8. Drink water

Water is important enough to deserve its own place on this list. Your voice needs water. Drink some as part of your pre-talk routine and make sure there is also some on the stage so you can reach for it whenever you need it.

That's you done!

Follow this checklist every time you are invited to speak and you will significantly increase the likelihood that your talk will go the way you planned.

Remember, this is all your responsibility. Do not expect the conference organiser or conference Chairperson to sort any of these things out for you. Take responsibility for them yourself. It is the only way to guarantee success.

Afterword – Hello mojo!

> "We cannot become
> what we want to be by
> remaining what we are."
>
> — MAX DEPREE —

Memorable, engaging public speakers are not born. They are ordinary people like you and me who make a conscious commitment to practising their public speaking technique, even when they think they no longer need to. The successful public speaker's enemies are not the people in the audience, colleagues or even failing technology. Our enemies are our complacency and our own negative self-talk.

If you take the time and care to practise using the mental rehearsal technique and get into your public speaking mindset using your pre-speaking routine you will give a wonderful, memorable presentation every single time.

Case study: Lauren's story**

While I was writing this book I was contacted by a 22-year-old lady called Lauren who was very worried. Lauren had been asked to read a poem at the funeral of a close friend in front of nearly a thousand mourners. I should think anyone would be daunted by the enormity of this task.

Lauren's main concern was that she would not be able to perform her duty because she would not be able to control her emotions. She was worried that her tears would prevent her from being able to say anything at all, let alone read a very sad poem!

I guided Lauren using many of the techniques that I have described in this book. In particular, the mental rehearsal technique described in Chapter 12 proved invaluable to her.

On the day after the funeral I received an email from Lauren. It read:

'Well, I did it! I felt so well-prepared I was actually excited and looking forward to going up! I delivered the poem well, clearly, at perfect pace with no stumbling or even the hint of a tear. I wish you could have seen! Many people approached me after the service and commented on how well I delivered the reading. I feel so proud to have contributed and even more so that I did it to a high standard – I definitely turned it up to eleven! The techniques you have taught me served me well today and

---

** Lauren is not her real name

will be invaluable for the future. I feel fantastic having done such a good job. You made a daunting task not only manageable but enjoyable and something to be proud of.'

I am so thrilled for Lauren and touched by her kind words about me. But as I reminded her, I did nothing. She was the one who took practice and preparation seriously. She was the one who found the strength within herself to believe that she could rise to this challenge in spite of her doubts. I hope you are as inspired by Lauren's story as I am.

It is now time for you to get your public speaking mojo back for good. The techniques described in this book have helped many of the people I work with in ways that have amazed both them and I. Start now. Give one of the exercises a go. Who knows where it may take you.

Now that you have read 'Get Your Public Speaking Mojo Back Forever!' I would love to hear how you find the tips and techniques in this book helpful. Which exercises work for you and which do not? Which sections of this book helped you and which parts left you cold?

Write to me at Julie@publicspeakingmojo.co.uk You can also visit www.publicspeakingmojo.co.uk for lots of additional resources including videos describing all the exercises in greater detail.

Now you know how to get your public speaking mojo back forever, what are you waiting for? See you on stage soon!

I want to work with you

When you bought this book you made a commitment to getting your public speaking mojo back. When you started reading this book you strengthened that commitment.

I now invite you to take the next big step forward and book a coaching session with me. Don't worry if you don't live in my area or think you would struggle to find the time. I am very happy to work with you over the internet using Skype.

Special offer

As a special offer and to thank you for investing in my book I would like to offer you a one-hour online coaching session for the very special price of just **£35.00**.

During the hour we will talk about where you would like to be and I will guide you through a number of recommended techniques to help you on your journey.

I can work at any time of day or night. So there really is no excuse! Be brave, and make an appointment with me now. To book, just go to my website at www.publicspeakingmojo.co.uk and enter the discount code **SKOFFER**

Bibliography & Resources

Anything you could possibly want but could not find in my book you will find in one of these highly enjoyable reads:

Cabane, Olivia Fox. The Charisma Myth: the art of personal magnetism. Portfolio Penguin, 2013.

Gladdish, Martin. The Lazy Optimist: Waking up from mediocrity and turning dreams into reality. Live It, 2013.

Lee, Stewart. How I Escaped my Certain Fate: the life and deaths of a stand-up comedian. Faber & Faber, 2011.

Lloyd-Hughes, Sarah. How to be Brilliant at Public Speaking: Any audience. Any situation. Pearson Life, 2011.

Lowndes, Leil. How to Talk to Anyone: 92 techniques for big success in relationships. Harper Element, 2014.

Ogunlaru, Rasheed. Soul Trader: Putting the heart back into your business. Kogan Page, 2012.

Peters, Prof. Steve. The Chimp Paradox: The mind management programme to help you achieve confidence, success and happiness. Vermilion, 2012.

Reilly, Lucas. 'Why Do Our Best Ideas Come to Us in the Shower?', mental_floss, 6th September 2013. http://mentalfloss.com/article/52586/why-do-our-best-ideas-come-us-shower

TIME. 'The Hidden Secrets of the Creative Mind', Time Magazine, 16th January 2006 http://content.time.com/time/magazine/article/0,917 1,1147152,00.html

Weinschenk, Susan. 'The Brain Science of Why Stepping Away Increases Creativity'. The Brain Lady Blog, 5th March 2015.
http://www.blog.theteamw.com/2014/03/05/the-brain-science-of-why-stepping-away-increases-creativity/

Williams, Nick. The Work you were Born to do: Find the work you love, love the work you do. Balloon View Ltd, 2010.

Wise, Anna. Awakening the Mind: A guide to mastering the power of your brain waves. Jeremy P. Tarcher, 2002.

If you have a fear of public speaking, the BPS website contains a list of counsellors who can help:

British Psychological Society www.BPS.org.uk

If you would like to find out more about mindfulness meditation, visit Anne Murray's website at www.annemurrayholistics.com

TED Talks, a treasure trove of brilliant talks www.ted.com

Acknowledgements

Murielle Maupoint and the rest of the team at Live It Publishing for making the pain of writing a pleasure.

David Stevenson aka 'Mr Julie' for enduring many months of tears, tantrums and self-doubt while I wrote this book, not to mention his invaluable technical support, endless patience and for feeding Derek* while I lived my dream of being a penniless writer.

Sheila Williamson for painstakingly proof-reading my early drafts, funding my ambition and giving birth to me.

Bill Thompson for writing this book's preface and for being a constant source of support and encouragement over many years.

Chris, Jenna, Stewart and Dan of digital agency Day Media, purveyors of many fine websites including my own.

Anne Murray for teaching me about mindfulness meditation and buying me hot chocolates when I was too poor to buy them for myself.

Bill Craig, my school English teacher who attempted to teach me to write well for four years. I'm proud that your efforts have at last borne fruit (but sorry for any poor grammar).

Martin Gladdish for introducing me to his publisher and urging me to write a book. If it wasn't for Martin you wouldn't be reading this. I like to think that's a good thing.

*my cat